YOUR CALLING

&

POSITIONING

Understanding Your Purpose & Sphere of Influence

Book # 2 From The "Seasoned For Destiny" Series

Sally Mahihu

Your Calling and Positioning

ISBN: 978-9914-9886-2-8

P. O. Box 4317-00200 Nairobi

Mobile No: 0722 820 969

Published in Kenya by

House of Wealth Publishers

+254 737 405 827

houseofwealthpublishers@gmail.com

Table of Contents

Chapter Ten

Chapter Eleven

Chapter Twelve

Dedication

I dedicate this book to every woman who desires to lay hold of her destiny but wonders how?

Acknowledgement

First and foremost, I would like to thank God for enabling me to write and finish this book series. I pray these books will impact and bless many Women who are determined to fulfil their destiny.

I would like to thank my **Husband Ngari** who really "gets me" and who I refer to as my "Destiny Spouse" because indeed he is a true gift from God and he has been supportive beyond measure during the course of my writing, these Books, in more ways than I can count.

My **sons Eric and Chris**, who are truly sons of my strength, and who have also supported and encouraged me in my "Destiny endeavours" no matter how radically insane I sounded at times.

My late **Dad, Chris Kahara** who constantly affirmed me and instilled the confidence I needed to embark on many "Destiny journeys" leading to where and who I am today.

Rev Teresa Wairimu, my "Destiny Midwife" who has spoken into my life for the past two decades and who has been diligent in nurturing, moulding and shaping me, to birth out the gifts within me (even during the times when my own foolishness and short-sightedness, coupled with a zeal that was often devoid of knowledge threatened to abort my Purpose and Calling.)

H.E. Madam Rachel Ruto who is equally passionate about the empowerment of women and who I admire and respect tremendously for her continuous and tireless commitment to better the lives of women in our society and Nation.

My Aunt Rev Judy Mbugua for believing in me and for being a pillar of strength to me for over the years as a Mother figure, for teaching me that my roles as a wife and mother are not an excuse for, but rather an incentive to fulfil my Purpose and Destiny.

My friend and Mentor Dr. Herta Von Stigel who came into my life, at just the right time and helped me to understand that I needed to conquer the Mountain within me before I could conquer the Mountains around me, and whose invaluable friendship and mentorship is a great source of encouragement for me.

My diligent research Assistants and Typists **Victor M. Mwangi**, **Frida Wanjira** and **Tecla Karimi** who all worked tirelessly in making these books happen.

My Publisher & Cover Designer Shadrack Radido of House Of Wealth Publishers who allowed me the freedom I needed in this Series of Books even when I stubbornly chose to deviate from the traditional Book writing ethics and who has been a solid sounding board on the many technical issues regarding this Series.

My Editor Dr. Mark Stibbe for his excellent editing and no-nonsense professional approach, truly a gift in the literary world.

My die-hard Spice Girls and faithful Women from my Seasoned Woman Vision who cheer me on and whose undeterred insistent claims that there is still more in me for them than I let out, warms my heart and provokes me to keep doing that which I was created for.

Everyone else who contributed in one way or another to the conception and birthing of this Series of Books.

Foreword

I have known Sally for over two decades now from the time she joined and begun to serve me in Ministry. Sally is a very zealous and passionate Woman in whatever she believes in.

Beyond her professional career as a Lawyer, Sally has demonstrated strong gifts of speaking, teaching, mentoring and writing and over the years I have often encouraged her to unleash these gifts. I am extremely proud to see that she has finally done so in these Books "**SEASONED FOR DESTINY**" and I am confident that she will go on to author many more for the benefit of this generation and the generations to come.

Sally has a distinct Call to the Women in the Marketplace for whom has an undeniable burden, and her ability to reach out and offer herself to those women who suffer in silence, totally closed up, yet they really need someone they can trust and open up to.

Sally has addressed every type of Woman in these Books and the topics and subjects she has chosen to address are of great interest so she will reach and impact a very wide margin of Women, across the divide, locally and globally.

In other words, Sally has covered literally every subject that every Woman needs, to become well equipped and empowered for fulfilling Purpose and Destiny. More importantly she has done it in a manner that every Woman will identify with, because she has delved into the core basics of every issue without sugar coating the seriousness that one will require to commit to this journey to Destiny. Yet at the same time she has strongly encouraged every Woman by laying out the roadmap and by affirming and assuring her again and again, that she already has what it takes to master this journey and fulfil her Destiny.

Women from every sphere and sector will be awakened to the significance of their Callings and Destiny, giving them the incentive and motivation, they needed to forge on without giving up.

I have been in Christian ministry for over 45 years now and I have been humbled and privileged to minister to thousands of people Worldwide and to lead an organization with over 10, 000 partners locally and globally. The messages in these Books are central to the gospel that I myself preach because Destiny is God ordained.

I have no doubt that everyone who will read these Books will be greatly impacted and transformed, empowered and equipped to arise and lay hold of and fulfil that Destiny that each was born for.

Rev. Teresia Wairimu Kinyanjui.

Director& Founder,

Faith Evangelistic Ministry (FEM).

Endorsement

Destiny is one of the most misunderstood concepts today. Needless to say, the very mention of this word elicits feelings of inadequacy and anxiety among many. This has mainly been because of the complexity and mystery that seems to surround the understanding of what destiny is or is not.

In the 'Seasoned for Destiny' series, Sally wholeheartedly deliberates on the tenets that are to bring flavor and color to one's life. Reading through the pages it is clear that she empties her heart seeking to touch a heart at a time. This series specifically address the internal struggles that become stumbling blocks in the way of success for many and in particular women.

In today's world where everything is fast-paced and we all are confronted with many options; it is prudent that one finds their space and balance in life. Reading this book will motivate you to take a personal stock of where you are in the journey to destiny while recognizing and fixing the hindrances on the way.

To live a life of meaning and significance understanding Destiny is not an option but an expectation. As one who is passionate about women empowerment, I concur that clarity of purpose and calling, the fortitude to make available connections and the resilience to maintain success on the path of destiny can be overwhelming. This series is therefore an essential tool for one to make this valuable journey.

Her Excellency,
Rachel Ruto.
Spouse of the Deputy President,
Republic of Kenya.

Endorsement

I have known Sally from when she was about 5 years old and our relationship is firstly that of a mother and daughter. Beyond our family ties and now that Sally has grown to be a wife and mother with her own home, we have become very close friends and prayer partners and we are a great support and strength to one another in this journey to Destiny.

From an early age, Sally has demonstrated such a strong gift of expression and articulation. Sally is undeniably a gifted and anointed Servant of God who ministers the gospel passionately. She is also an inspirational coach and mentor to many women and girls from every walk of life. Her marketplace ministry has impacted many far and wide.

When Sally birthed her Seasoned Woman Forum about 7 years ago and as I witnessed her teachings, mentorship and coaching programs, I knew it would just be a matter of time before she consolidated those valuable teachings into books to reach a wider audience and sphere.

I think that every woman reading this book who will be transformed radically and propelled to fulfilling her Purpose and Destiny.

I am very passionate for Families and Nations, and a firm believer that strong healthy families are the foundation of strong healthy Nations. So, as I read these Books, I was deeply affected and encouraged by the manner in which Sally has tied up the value of the woman, not only as a leader, wealth creator, professional, career woman, but also as a family-oriented woman.

Any woman serious about fulfilling her Purpose and Destiny must be able to align her role as a family woman with her Purpose and Destiny and she must be cognizant of the fact that she cannot effectively impact Nations without first impacting families.

This series of books addresses every woman of every race, creed and color, and from any society and Nation, who desires to be and do all that she was born and created for.

Sally has adequately highlighted literally every dilemma and problem that a woman will encounter in the course of fulfilling her Purpose and Destiny, irrespective of her social status and standing in life, and she has given very practical solutions to these dilemmas and problems.

I would therefore urge every woman to read this Series of Books not only for her own equipping and empowerment but also for the equipping and empowerment of other women who she will share the contents of these book with.

Rev. Dr Judy Mbugua.

The Founder of the Homecare Spiritual Fellowship.

Endorsement

Sally Mahihu's book series "Seasoned for Destiny" is a clarion call for every woman, regardless of age, race or tribe, to discover her true identity, live out her deeper purpose and leave a legacy that younger generations are proud to remember. This book series is for such as time as this!"

(**Dr Herta von Stiegel,** author of "*The Mountain Within – Leadership Lessons and Inspiration for your Climb to the Top.*")

Endorsement

I am glad that Sally has followed through in writing this series of books titled "Seasoned for Destiny". A couple of years ago, I gave her a word which I had received from the lord, that she would write some very significant books on issues pertaining to women in the marketplace.

These books will encourage and guide women greatly in understanding certain fundamentals that are related to their destiny such as business, career, leadership, relationships etc. Sally has captured literally every aspect of a modern woman's life, and she has taken time to address and analyze these issues in a way that every woman can identify with.

Sally has left no stone unturned in candidly addressing the subtle and not so subtle issues that often derail and delay many women from unleashing their full potential, to enable them to bring out their best selves.

I am persuaded that these books will change the lives of many women and will equip a new generation to become powerful agents of transformation in their spheres of influence.

Rev. Steve Pailthorpe

President of Crown Global, CEO of Iconic Digital & Senior Pastor of Crown Family Church

Introduction

I am fully persuaded that once a Woman understands who she was born to be and embraces the reason she was created (the Purpose for her being), then she will begin to live purposefully and intentionally towards it, and attain true fulfilment. And in so doing she will not only lay hold of her own Destiny, but she will also impact and propel many people, societies and Nations to their Purpose and Destiny as well.

This Series known as **"SEASONED FOR DESTINY"** consists of 5 Books namely Book 1 Your Naming and Defining, Book 2 Your Calling And Positioning, Book 3 Your Relationships And Networks, Book 4 Your Making And Shaping and Book 5 Your Harvests And Legacy.

Book 1 Titled "**Your Naming And Defining**" deals with a Woman's identity, understanding **"the who"** she was born to be, it addresses her ability to embrace her true and authentic self. The chapters in this Book expound the various fundamentals regarding Identity and the power of Naming; The Passwords to your true identity (understanding what should and what should not define you). The Triggers to an Identity Crisis, The Diary of a Destiny Diva, The Voices that shape and define you, The Destiny Queen or the Destiny Quitter, The Destiny Preserver or the Destiny Destroyer, The Destiny Clinger or the Destiny Kisser, The Destiny Connector or the Destiny Blocker, The Global Destiny Carrier or the Local Destiny Carrier, The Destiny Respecter or the Destiny Despiser, The Eagle Destiny or the Chicken Destiny, The Diary of a Destiny Diva and The Daily Confessions of a Destiny Chaser (on how to reinforce and affirm your identity daily with positive decrees and declarations).

Book 2 Titled "**Your Calling And Positioning**" deals with a Woman's Calling and Purpose namely how to discover "**the what**" she was created to do, how to birth it and safeguard it, having a deep insight of what her purpose and calling entails, understanding how to access what she needs to fulfil it. This Book also it looks at the Woman's Positioning and Alignment on how to locate "**the where**" (in terms of sector or sphere) she is ordained to impact, how to navigate in that specific area and how to establish herself there. The chapters in this particular Book address the pertinent factors about Calling and Positioning namely; The Cues and Clues to her Calling, The Realities About her Calling, The Tools of a true Visionary, The steps to Birthing her Visions to Destiny, The Steps after Birthing her Visions to Destiny, The Pebble Stones in your High Heels to Destiny, The Arrows to her Place and sphere, The Snags and Snares in her Place and sphere, Establishing herself in the Place of Assignment and The Key Roles Of A Destiny Woman.

Book 3 Titled "**Your Relationships And Networks**" deals with a Woman's relationships (networks and associations) namely "**the whom**" she should connect to, or disconnect from, for the sake of her Destiny. The chapters in this Book address; The Paradoxes In A Destiny Woman, Your Destiny Helpers, Your Destiny Killers, Your Sibling Rivals, Mastering

The Art of Negotiation, The Spice Girls and Your Suspect Suitors.

Book 4 Titled "**Your Making And Shaping**" deals with a Woman's moulding and sculpturing for Destiny namely "**the How**" of her preparation and equipping, and the various tests and trials she needs to undergo in order to fulfil her Purpose and Call as well as the principles, values and habits that inform her choices and decisions and refine her for Destiny. The chapters in this Book address and include; The Storms of a Destiny Survivor, The Scars of a Sculptured Woman, The Pain Patterns of a Destiny Champion, The Shape of a Destiny Diamond, The Trademarks of a Destiny Vessel, The Habits of a Destiny Addict, The Elegance of an Eagle Woman and The Pitstops of a Destiny Racer.

Book 5 Titled "**Your Harvests And Legacy**" deals with a Woman's legacy and the footprints she leaves behind for her generation and future generations. The chapters in this Book include; The Seasons Of a Destiny Sower, Your Harvest In 7 Areas, Facts About Your Harvest, Hindrances To Your Harvest, Threats To Your Harvest, How To Respond To Your Harvest, Reasons Why You Get The Harvest, The Purpose Of Your Harvest, The Marks Of A Destiny Legend and A Woman's Defining Decades.

One of the main reasons for writing this Book was to consolidate the principles that I have been teaching, coaching and mentoring on over the years with regard to Purpose and Destiny.

Perhaps another compelling reason for writing this Series of Books is that every issue addressed here resonates within me personally, because these are issues I or people very close to me, continue to grapple with, and my sharing them here is for purposes of identifying my own personal struggles with those of the women I am addressing.

It is my sincere desire and hope that those who read this Series of Books will use the teachings to propel themselves to Destiny and to pass them on to other women, including those they are training, mentoring and coaching.

These Books will also form very valuable material for discussion groups whether as Book clubs, diverse groups within churches, corporate organizations and in all the various sectors and spheres of influence and hence the reason I have inserted "Destiny questions to ponder on" at the end of each chapter so that the interactive discussions can have a real impact on each reader and hopefully provoke them to apply the guidelines offered here in fulfilling their Purpose and Calling.

My sincere hope and expectation is that these Books are going to equip and empower every Woman desirous of fulfilling Purpose and to edify and assure her that no matter how hard the journey has been and no matter how much she has wanted to give up, she indeed has what it takes to finish this journey because she was designed for Destiny and she is already seasoned for it.

Although the target audience of this Series is primarily Women, it is now clear to me that even the men who come across them it will be equally impacted and equipped by the universal principles and the various topics addressed.

It is also my intention to target the young woman (older teens and young adults) because most of these principles and issues will greatly help these young women to avoid the mistakes that many of us older women made in our early years, and it will hopefully help the young woman to also avoid unnecessary delays in her journey to Destiny. It is therefore my sincere hope and prayer that every woman, young and old will read this Series of Books and be propelled to her Destiny.

The most fundamental aspect when embarking on your journey to Destiny is knowing "the **who you were born to be**" and coming to a place where you embrace your true and authentic self and walk securely in it because everything else thereafter regarding your Destiny hinges on this first revelation about your true self-identity.

These Books address, every Woman at whatever place she may be in her quest for Purpose and Destiny, the late Destiny bloomer, the Destiny dreamer and Destiny chaser, the Destiny wagon, the Destiny spectator, the Destiny backslider.

These Women are all desirous of living purposefully but they each struggle with different aspects about Destiny, whereby some may struggle with knowing and discovering '**the who**' and '**the what**' they were created to be (their self-identity and Calling), they go round in circles seeking '**the where**' they were assigned to influence (their place and sphere of assignment) and '**the whom**' they were designed to relate and connect with (the relationships), many of them get blindsided by the how they get made and formed (tests, trials and tribulations), while others navigate life steering dangerously without a road map seeking '**the which**' (values and principles) they need to get there, while others become lethargic and burnout because they lack a sufficient conviction that the journey is worth the high price and sacrifice, they seem to be paying.

Every Woman's future after reading this Series of Books will be brightened by her assurance and confidence that she can now become the who she was born to be, do the what she was created to do, locate and position herself where she was sent to be an influence, relate and connect with the people that were assigned for her, surrender and embrace the process that will mould and make her into a vessel fit for Destiny, walk and align with the principles and values that she was intended to use to usher her to Destiny, lay hold of and effectively manage the successes, rewards and harvests that come with her faithfulness and diligence and leave footprints that will be a positive legacy for her generation and future generations.

WHAT IS TO BE SEASONED FOR DESTINY?

For Purposes of this series of Books being "**Seasoned**" does not mean you have accomplished and "**arrived**" rather it means that you are passionate enough to lay hold of your Destiny, that you are ready to step forth by faith and embark on this epic journey just as you are; with the assurance that as you do so, the equipping and empowering you seek or need will be part and parcel of the journey.

… "**Being Seasoned for Destiny**" means that even though you occasionally struggle with who you are in the midst of a tumultuous dispensation that often seeks to swallow and drown you… **YET** you tenaciously fight to keep your head up, knowing that there is only one of you, and the only one you need to be, the one you were born to be.

… "**Being Seasoned for Destiny**" means that even though there are many raw and rough edges in your Character, that are still undergoing moulding and shaping… **YET** you continue to submit yourself to the skillful hands of the Master Potter, knowing that a "**Choice Vessel**" like you, will take longer to be formed because of the great impact and influence you will have on Nations and Generations.

... **"Being Seasoned for Destiny"** means that even though you have not quite mastered the Storms of life like failed relationships, chronic failures, loneliness, self-doubt and rejection, just to mention a few... **YET** you continue to brace yourself against those storms, choosing to dance in the rain; knowing that as you continue to set your sail in the wind of hope then ultimately, those storms will in fact become the very forces that will strengthen and propel you and bring you to that higher place of being alone, but not lonely, a place of self-knowledge, self-acceptance and self-assurance.

.... **"Being Seasoned for Destiny"** means that even though the seed of your womb has not germinated into the **"Daughters of Substance"** and **"Sons of Strength"** you had hoped for... **YET** you remain expectant that irrespective of any shortcomings in your parenting skills, or any unjust twist of fate, your resilience as a praying mother is never in vain and in due season, your Sons and Daughters will manifest into a Seasoned Generation, that will shake cities and impact Nations.

... **"Being seasoned for Destiny"** means that even though you may constantly be in a financial mess and distress, until you feel so desperate and drained... **YET** you refuse to despair knowing that your hands are anointed to create wealth and as you continue to trust, embrace and practice sound godly wealth creating habits and principles, then surely the floodgates of heaven will fling open and usher you into unprecedented financial freedom.

... **"Being Seasoned for Destiny "** means that even though the dire consequences of your **poor choices**, have come to haunt you and you are paying the painful price of your past folly under a heavy cloak of remorse... **YET** you keep your head lifted up high knowing that as you appreciate the lessons learned from your past folly, then this too will pass; because your harsh and ugly Winter must ultimately surrender to your soft and beautiful Spring that will come with forbearance and Second Chances.

… **"Being Seasoned for Destiny"** means that perhaps your inner joy is being dampened by the anguish and agony of a sick body…. **YET** you forge on, smiling through your pain knowing that as long as you have a Purpose and Assignment, that you are committed to fulfil and a Destiny to lay hold of, then your Creator will preserve you and keep you, until you are done.

…**"Being Seasoned for Destiny"** means that even though your walk with God is like a seesaw, characterised by some seasons of intense (almost fanatical) passion and commitment and a radical faith, but also with other seasons of panic, doubt, or even silent indignation when things do not go the way you thought… **YET** you pick yourself up every time and dust off the doubt and purge your panic, and with hot blinding tears, you make a decision to hope and trust anyway, knowing that He who began a good work in you is able to complete it.

…**"Being Seasoned For Destiny"** means that even though you have encountered Chronic failures and disappointment… **YET** it is about finding the grace to deal with the many disappointments of life and finding the resolve to regain missed seasons and lost opportunities, it is about finding the strength to reposition yourself for a new beginning, because a Seasoned Woman knows, that while there is life, there is hope and while there is hope, there is always another chance to rise again and forge on to fulfil her Destiny.

… **"Being Seasoned for Destiny"** means that even though you come to the end of yourself **YET** your find a song in your heart that keeps you going when the journey gets tough and this is the song that will keep her going even when the storms rage and the fiery furnace flares.

The Seasoned Woman knows…

Who she really is…

The Purpose for which she was created…

She is uniquely gifted…

She does not allow her failures…

And successes to define her…

She confidently says…

When I grow up I want to be Me!

The Seasoned Woman knows…

She is fearfully and wonderfully made…

With a true beauty inside her…

Reflected in her whole life lived…

The Seasoned Woman clothes herself…

In dignity, honesty, integrity, patience, kindness, mercy and love…

The Seasoned Woman has learnt…

To embrace the seasons of her life…

Allow them to mould and sculpt her…

Into a vessel of strength, honour and dignity…

She is a Woman of all Seasons...
A vessel of strength, honour and dignity...

She has learnt to weather and survive the storms of her daily life...
Having the grace to dance in the rain...
To smile through her pain...

She has risen to define life...
The strength to rise like a phoenix from the ashes...

The Seasoned Woman has passion for her Nation...
She has solutions for her Generation...
And she has the welfare of her people at heart...
She is a voice to the voiceless...

So, as you reflect and take stock of all the myriad of Seasons you may have encountered so far in your journey to Destiny, remember that you are **"So Totally Seasoned"** for your Destiny and that nothing shall by any means prevent you, from finishing your Race and not only finishing it, but finishing strong... so soldier on **Woman of Destiny**, until you reach the finish line.

Chapter One

Chosen For Destiny

Understanding The Power Of Your Purpose

Chapter Preview

1. *Your Calling and Destiny is Predetermined*

2. *Your Calling and Destiny is a Choice*

3. *Your Calling and Destiny is Tailor-Made for You*

4. *Your Calling and Destiny Comes with a Cost and a Sacrifice*

5. *Your Daily Activities, Goals and Visions should Align with Your Calling and Destiny*

6. *Your Calling and Destiny will Involve a Process and Struggles*

7. *Your Priorities Determine your Destiny*

1. YOUR CALLING AND DESTINY IS PREDETERMINED

Destiny is that which you were predetermined to do and become so that you reach to an expected end.

"For I know the thoughts that I think towards you, saith the Lord, thoughts of peace and not Evil, to give you an expected end." Jere.29:11

Your Calling is the key to your life and without it, your life has no meaning. Your Destiny is what you were ordained to be in life, your expected end. There is a book of Destiny written about each one of us (Psalms 139:16).

"There is no greater gift you can give or receive than to honour your Calling. It is why you were born and how you become most truly alive." **Oprah Winfrey**

We have been predestined according to purpose. Destiny is the blue print of your life.

Our destiny is not guess work or something we make up as we go along, God had planned it before we were born, he worked out the course that our lives will take and it's up to us to accept and embrace it.

2. FULFILLING YOUR CALLING AND DESTINY IS A CHOICE

Your destiny is your choice, master your destiny, you alone decides if to fulfil it by your decisions and actions

In other words, your Calling will guide your life choices and decisions, it will influence your behaviour, habits, it will shape your goals, Visions and dreams etc.

"Destiny is not a matter of chance, it is a matter of choice, and it is not a thing to be waited for but a thing to be achieved." **William Jennings Bryan**

Our choices and decisions determine our Destiny not our conditions or our circumstances.

"It is your moments of decisions that your destiny is shaped." By Anthony Robbins

3. YOUR CALLING AND DESTINY IS TAILOR-MADE FOR YOU

Our destiny is tailor-made for us and we are unique for our purpose. Like the master of a ship heads into a harbour, God uses many different buoys and ways to guide us into our destiny and stay on course; by his word, by his presence, by his decrees in us, by our inner witness, by the inner voice of our spirit, wise counsel from wise men, by provision (when he guides, he provides).

Your Calling that you were created for is that which you are extremely and deeply motivated by, or that which you love to do and you have a natural grace and flare for. You will have a deep passion for what you were born to do.

Your Destiny is like a glove, tailor-made to fit you perfectly. So do not worry and fret how it will come together.

Do not envy the Callings and Destinies of others, because they are meant for them and yours is meant for you. Do not compete or force their shoe to fit your foot, because you not only get blisters trying.

Jim Collins, in his book *From Good to Great*, writes about the hedgehog concept which he explains as being based on three key elements. These are:

- *What you are deeply passionate about*
- *What you can be best at in the world and*
- *What you can profit from*

According to Jim Collins, once these three elements are aligned, you are in the centre of the Calling for which you were created.

God uses every situation in your life to help shape you for your Destiny. According to Psalm 139, God designed you in His image, with a unique DNA and amazing characteristics; created for a purpose that only can fulfil.

You must therefore find your own sense of belonging and the path to becoming the original authentic version of you that God intended.

4. YOUR CALLING AND DESTINY COMES WITH A COST AND SACRIFICE

Pursuing Destiny will often entail, leaving everything you know and hold dear (whether it a place, things, people etc.) to pursue your Destiny, to go and become what you were created to become. Letting go means that you come to a realization that some places, things and people are part of your history and not part of your destiny.

Your Destiny is waiting for you to pay the price but it will be worth the effort.

As Steve Maraboli says, *"Don't let your history interfere with your Destiny."* This means that you should stop being a victim of your circumstances and start taking action towards the life you were created for. Break free from the poisonous victim mentality and embrace the truth of your greatness. You have what it takes to shape your life and fulfil your Destiny.

5. YOUR DAILY ACTIVITIES, GOALS AND VISIONS SHOULD ALIGN WITH YOUR CALLING AND DESTINY

Measure what you do according to what God has created you to do. Check your activities in terms of how they help you fulfil your Destiny. You are a master piece, special, rare, unique, valuable, named, known, called and chosen.

A Calling is 'the why' each one of us was created and it will entail accomplishing certain tasks and assignments for the greater goal of human kind, in terms of impacting and transforming lives and places positively and fulfilling God's plan and agenda on the earth.

Our Calling is what we are supposed to do in life. You are a person of Destiny, you are equipped, you are talented, you are creative, and you are designed for a specific purpose.

6. YOUR CALLING AND DESTINY WILL INVOLVE A PROCESS AND A STRUGGLE

The process towards stepping into our Destiny has hardships and struggles as you move forward into the Destiny that God has for you. God is not interested in our comfort, if he has to, he will shake things up to fit us to Destiny. God's plan cannot be stopped by any force of darkness. No one can keep you from your Destiny. No one can stop your Destiny. God knows how to get us where we need to be. God knows the end from the beginning, the mistakes we will make etc. so he calculates for contingences.

"Hardships, often prepare ordinary people for an extraordinary destiny." **By CS Lewis**

Your Destiny is not the end, it is the entire journey. Fulfilling your Destiny is a process which entails a Calling, a preparation and a commissioning.

"You don't know the whole future, you don't see the full picture forward but take a step of faith, don't lean on your own understanding, "Destiny is a journey, a process." Unknown

7. YOUR PRIORITIES DETERMINE YOUR DESTINY

Discovering and fulfilling your Calling and Destiny should be the most important thing in your life.

"Our greatest fear should not be of failure but of succeeding at things in life that don't really matter." **Francis Chan**

Anything else you may accomplish and succeed in will be of no consequence if you fail to fulfil your Call and Destiny that God created you for.

"Your life has a Purpose, your story is important, your dreams count, your voice matters, you were born to make an impact." *Unknown*

In your journey to Destiny some of the key things, will be finding the cues and clues to discovering your Calling, seeing the spot – lights that will point you towards it, finding the tool kit for fulfilling it, understanding the steps to birthing it, and the steps after birthing it, acknowledging the gravel stones in your high heels that will seek to slow you down towards your Destiny, balancing and managing the different roles in your life that will often seek to compete with your Destiny etc.

Destiny Questions To Ponder On

1. *What is your understanding of predestination?*

2. *Do you believe you have made the right choices to lead you to your Calling and Destiny?*

3. *Are you convinced that your Calling and Destiny is tailor-made for you? Why?*

4. *What costs and sacrifices have you made so far for your Calling and Destiny?*

5. *Which of your daily or regular activities do you feel do not align to your Calling and Destiny?*

6. *How would you describe the process you have undergone so far in fulfilling your Calling and Destiny?*

7. *Do you believe that you have prioritized your Calling and Destiny?*

Chapter Two

Cues & Clues
To Your Calling

The Signals That Define Your Calling

Chapter Preview

1. *A Promise from God about something*

2. *A Passion and love for something*

3. *A Pain or burden for something*

4. *A Magnetic Pull towards something*

5. *A Power and Authority over something*

6. *A Potential within you for something*

7. *A Problem to Solve concerning something*

OPENING REMARKS

Some of the spot-lights and pointers that will lead you into discovering your Calling will be clues such as a **promise** or a dream that you have in your heart, a **passion** and intense love for something, a **pain** or a burden for something or a situation, a magnetic **pull** towards something, a **power** within you to accomplish that thing, a **potential** within you comprising of gifts, talents and skills for that thing, and a **problem** you discern and that you are able to solve etc.

If you want to know what you are gifted for check what people are constantly asking you for.

1. A PROMISE

"From one end of the Bible to the other, God assures us that He will never go back on His promises". Billy Graham

He who has called you and pre-determined your Calling will have given you a promise about your Calling, the impact it will have, and His unconditional support in enabling and equipping you until you successfully fulfil it, and that promise will be a crucial pointer in directing and guiding you to discover and lock into your Calling and Destiny.

In other words, God does the promising and then we fulfil the Calling He has given us in order to lay hold of that promise.

2. A PASSION

"If you cannot figure out your Purpose, figure out your passion. For your passion will lead you right into your Purpose." **Bishop T.D Jakes.**

What is it that you are so passionate about, and you love deeply and enjoy doing and more so, you do it so easily or it comes so easily to you?

Your passion is almost uncontrollable and can often consume you, so it is like a good obsession, that many around you may not understand and some may even judge and criticize you for it. It is a deep and vibrant excitement for something, usually a cause, a Vision or a dream that you passionately immerse yourself in and desire to see it fulfilled.

Your passion could also be an intense and strong desire against something that you are deeply opposed to. You feel a deep desire to eradicate it or remove it from around you or your society because you see it as unhealthy, harmful and destructive towards people you love and care for. Passion is one of the key pointers to discovering your Calling. That passion will keep you alive, rejuvenate, energize and resurrect you and revive the gifting, talent and skills within you and unleash your potential to its fullness.

"Purpose is the reason you journey and passion is what lights the way." **Unknown**

Your passion is the fuel for fulfilling your Calling. It will reinforce the strengths within you and make you acknowledge and appreciate them and use them to their full maximum. It will also make you aware of the weaknesses within you and enable you to manage those weaknesses. In other words, your passion and love for your Calling will make you feed your strengths and starve your weaknesses.

Your passion motivates you and it is the reason you wake up every morning. It is the reason you get up every time you fall and it is the reason you refuse to accept failures. It is the reason you choose to adopt a positive attitude and lifestyle and to resist every attempt by people and your enemies to silence you into inaction.

"When your passion and Purpose are greater than you then you will find a way." ~ **Unknown**

3. A PAIN

The things that burden you and grieve you (for example poverty, hunger sickness, ignorance, disorganization corruption, abuse, injustice, oppression etc.) are key pointers to discovering your Calling because those are probably the things you were born to correct and heal.

It is a weight that weighs heavily on you and it will only lift once you have done the needful by stepping into the situation and taking the action required to correct and heal that thing or situation.

"Believe that there is a Purpose in your pain." Kay Warren

A burden will provoke you into action, whereby you cannot restrain yourself. It will not matter that you may not have the support, resources and backing that you need. You will often take radical steps of faith and fortunately you will find that the support, resources and backing will catch up with you.

In other words, your burden to correct and heal that situation will not be deterred by any limitations and you will wade through and overcome every obstacle in your way.

You will need to acknowledge and respect that burden within you. Any attempts to ignore it or suppress it will only cause you more pain and more grievance and the burden will not lift or disappear just because you have ignored it. Fortunately, there will always be strategies for you to address that pain and burden within you. All you need to do is seek and adopt those strategies so that as you implement and execute them, that burden within you will be released.

As the painful burden begins to lift off of you, it is a sign that you are effectively fulfilling your Calling, and addressing the situations that you were created to address and deal with. It will be a sign that you are unleashing your full potential into providing answers for problems in your society and nation and providing solutions to the dilemmas of those people around you.

The mistake of ignoring or seeking to suppress a God given burden within you, may ultimately silence you and make dormant the gifts, talents and skills that were already within you unless you decide to acknowledge that burden and pain. It is like a cross that you must bear and have victory over.

"God often uses our deepest pain as the launching pad of our greatest Calling." **Unknown**

4. A MAGNETIC PULL

"Your Destiny is like a magnet constantly pulling you towards it." **T. D Jakes**

That which you are strongly drawn towards is a key pointer and indicator to discovering your Calling because you are drawn to that which you are called for. You will inevitably notice and pay attention to that which you were created to do. So that there are things others around you may not notice or see because those things are not their assignment, but you will be magnetically pulled and drawn towards those things. So your Calling is like a magnet it attracts all that you need for your Destiny.

Resisting the magnetic pull towards your Calling will leave you restless, frustrated, stressed and unfulfilled. The worst thing to live with is a void and an emptiness that comes as a result of not being in the centre of the Calling for which you were created.

The magnetic pull will also be towards things that are related to your Calling such as a desire for certain skills, competencies etc. In other words, you will enjoy studying and learning, researching and reading about things that are related to your Calling.

That magnetic pull will attract you towards your Calling and will also draw you to the relationships and people who are intended and ordained to help you fulfil your Calling. It will pull you also towards those people who you are ordained to influence, transform and impact as you fulfil your Calling, otherwise known as the people of your Calling.

That Magnetic pull towards your Calling will repel you away from anything that contradicts your Calling or anything and anyone who fights that Calling or seeks to destroy and kill that Calling. Those things and those people are essentially the enemies of your Destiny.

Instead that Magnetic pull will draw you towards the place of your Calling and into your Place of Assignment, because your Calling must be fulfilled in a certain place (whether geographically or symbolically) where the atmosphere and environment is conducive and where you have a special grace and anointing to thrive and be productive.

5. A POWER

"There is nothing so powerful as a human with a Purpose."
Unknown

Your Calling will be a powerful force and authority within you that motivates you and keeps you going like a super natural energy. As long as you are doing that thing, you don't get as tired, exhausted or bored and you can go on for hours, in other words when you have a unique grace for that thing, then you know it is your Calling.

Another key pointer to discovering your Calling is by analyzing that which you are so good at that you could easily be the best in the world at it.

"When your life is in course with its Purpose, you are at your most powerful. And though you may stumble, you will not fall" Oprah Winfrey

You must examine yourself and ascertain what are your powers, strengths, skills and competences that others will readily pay for (which they obviously view as very valuable and worth paying for). In addition, they trust those skills and competences within you to deliver what they need from you.

You must also constantly examine yourself and check what captivates your mind and spirit. What do you spend most of your time thinking and deliberating about or what consumes or obsesses you in a positive way. What do you find yourself talking most about to other people because that is a clue as to what power occupies your heart and mind.

Also look out for what people see and acknowledge as your gifts and ability and the things that they say you are good at. Check what they often commend and appreciate you for. Your true Calling cannot remain hidden from those around you and their perception will often be a confirmation of what you already know about yourself and your Calling.

It is also crucial for you to check what you are powerful at and you have authority over. What you do so easily and yet it turns a profit whether or not you intended it to. Fulfilling your true Calling will inevitably generate some valuable returns for you, others, your society and nation.

6. A POTENTIAL

"Potential is a priceless treasure, like gold. All of us have gold hidden within, but we have to dig to get it out." Joyce Meyer

This is where you have latent abilities within you gifts and talents that somehow unleash and manifest whenever you are in your Calling. In other words, those latent abilities within you are awaiting for you to engage in your Calling so that they become fully blown and manifested.

Unfortunately, some people fail to unleash their potential for fulfilling their Purpose due to a lack of self-awareness (meaning an insufficient self-knowledge in terms of their identity their strengths and weaknesses). Also due to a lack of motivation towards their Calling or a complete lack of revelation and failure to discover it. Sometimes it is simply due to focusing on the wrong attributes and qualities within themselves instead of focusing on unleashing those attributes and qualities necessary for their Purpose and Calling.

"There is no heavier burden than an unfulfilled potential." **Charles M. Schulz**

The potential within you is the unrealized ability and capacity that needs to be unleashed to enable you fulfil your Call and

Destiny. It shows you have what it takes, but you must be willing to unleash it and use it by making the right decisions and choices, taking the right steps and actions and engaging in the right activities.

"Our potential lies between what is and what could be." **Kim Butley**

Unleashing your potential includes appreciating, knowing and feeding your strengths, gifts, talents and skills harnessing and sharpening them. It also includes acknowledging, starving and managing your weaknesses so that they do not overshadow your strengths. It means working on your character, developing the right habits, attitudes and mind-sets that will enhance and empower you in fulfilling your Purpose and Calling.

The potential within you will be a clear pointer to what your Purpose and Calling is because that potential will reveal certain attributes, capabilities etc. that align with that Purpose.

7. A PROBLEM TO SOLVE

"Life is a continuous exercise in creative problem solving." **Michael J. Gelb**

Your Calling will be an answer to a problem and a solution to someone's dilemma or in a situation or sector, industry or sphere in your society and nation.

There is someone right now who needs the rare gift of your time, beauty, energy or material resources.

Your Calling is a reward to your people, society and nation. This means that there will be a targeted group of people or community who will be the beneficiaries of your Calling. Needless to say, your Calling will be geared towards filling a gap and addressing and confronting an issue or issues that are awaiting for you. The problems and dilemmas that your Calling solves are a matter of life and death to a people or a society or a nation.

The answers and solutions that your Calling provide, cannot be easily seen by others who are not called to do what you are called to do. That's why your Calling makes you a solution provider to your generation and the future generations and delivers the people, society and nations from destruction.

"Leaders are problem solvers by talent and temperament, and by choice." **Harlan Cleveland**

Another key pointer to discovering your Calling is seeing what you flow in effortlessly and with such an abundance of grace.

You will have a grace to solve problems and dilemmas that others find extremely distressful difficult and cumbersome. Yet to you it is the most important task and assignment in which you see a lot of value and therefore you give it your all.

"Position yourself as a listener and a problem solver." Unknown

You will easily thrive at something that others find so difficult to get a breakthrough in. You will be able to unravel and solve problems and dilemmas with a special kind of ability etc.

You will enjoy doing something that others loathe doing yet to you it is the most enjoyable and pleasant thing you find doing.

You will have a supernatural enablement to do something that ordinarily you would not be able to do naturally. It is a special endowment within you which is God given, specifically to enable you fulfil your Calling.

You will see potential and resources in a situation that others cannot see, because of your passion and devotion to your Calling. You are more likely to get divine revelation and insight and to see availability of resources and other tools you need to fulfil that Calling even where others are blinded and cannot see what you see (because their passion is not for that Calling).

You will find strategies within you to handle things effectively and efficiently to the amazement of those around you. In fact, you will become so sharp intellectually, emotionally and mentally that you will be able to grasp complicated issues and decipher and apply knowledge and information beyond your normal capacity.

"Running away from any problem only increases the distance from the solution. The easiest way to escape from a problem is to solve it."
Unknown

Destiny Questions to Ponder On

1. *How did God communicate his promise to you about your Calling, was it through a dream, a person or just an insight?*

2. *What is the one thing you have noticed that has a tendency to kill your passion for your Calling?*

3. *What pains and burdens you?*

4. *What magnetically pulls you away from your Calling and how do you resist that magnet?*

5. *Are the three elements of the hedgehog concept aligned as regards your Calling?*

6. *Is there some potential within you that you sense has not yet been unleashed towards your Calling, what do you think hinders the unleashing of that potential?*

7. *What specific problem do you believe that your Calling solves in your society and nation?*

This Page Was Intentionally Left Blank

Chapter Three

The Realities About Your Calling

Knowing What Your Calling Entails

Chapter Preview

1) Your Calling is your Reason for Living

2) Your Calling is a Gift to Mankind

3) Your Calling Will Preserve You

4) Your Calling Has a Process

5) Your Calling Has a Place

6) Your Calling Has Seasons

7) Your Calling Will Cost You

OPENING REMARKS

Knowing what your Calling is all about will greatly help you in embarking on it full heartedly. Consequently, you will need to be attentive in understanding all the facts concerning your Calling so that you are adequately equipped and prepared in fulfilling it. The word of God will be key in helping you understand facts about your Calling. In addition, any relevant information and knowledge that you will acquire from your Destiny helpers and Destiny connectors.

It's Not How You Begin, It's How You Finish

Whether you were born with a **"silver spoon"** or with a **"metal spade"** in your mouth, you are a child of Destiny, and you have an equal opportunity to fulfil your Destiny.

So, while we applaud the **"rags to riches"** story, we should also applaud the **"riches to riches"** story because while one strove to make it, the other strove to maintain it and sustain it.

Sometimes the maintaining and sustaining, is harder than the making. So, it's really not how you begin, but it's about how you finish and more importantly, it is the impact and the influence you make and the legacy you leave for the future generations.

1. YOUR CALLING IS YOUR REASON FOR LIVING

As long as you are still alive, there is still a Purpose for your life. We were created to fulfil God's plan on earth and he has prepared specific works for us to walk in.

Ephesians 2:10 – *"For we are His workmanship, created in Christ Jesus for good works, which God prepared beforehand that we should walk in them."*

He has incredible valuable tasks for us to carry out which were designed uniquely for us. We are made specifically, intentionally and perfectly in line with our ordained tasks. Each person is fit for their Purpose and call.

We must be worthy of the Calling with which we were called

Ephesians 4:1-6 – *"I, therefore, the prisoner of the Lord, beseech you to walk worthy of the Calling with which you were called, with all lowliness and gentleness, with longsuffering, bearing with one another in love, endeavouring to keep the unity of the Spirit in the bond of peace. There is one body and one Spirit, just as you were called in one hope of your Calling; one Lord, one faith, one baptism; one God and Father of all, who is above all, and through all, and in you all."*

So, we have no time to do our own will, we are here to do God's will. This means that we must subject every decision regarding our jobs, roles, marriage, relationships, business etc. to ensure they align with God's plan and will for us.

"There is no greater gift you can give or receive than honour your Calling. It's why you were born and how you become truly alive." **Unknown**

Everyone has a Calling and your Calling was pre-ordained, so your Calling is aligned to God's agenda for mankind.

This therefore presupposes that your unwillingness to discover your Calling or your failure or refusal to embark on fulfilling it for whatever reasons disqualifies you from living. So, discovering and fulfilling your Calling is not voluntary or optional. It is a mandatory mandate.

"You don't decide what your Purpose is in life you discover it. Your Purpose is your reason for living." Bob Proctor

2. YOUR CALLING IS A GIFT TO MANKIND

"The best way to find yourself is to lose yourself in the service of others." ~ **Mahatma Gandhi**

Your Calling is God's gift to you, fulfilling it is your gift to God and mankind.

Your Calling is intended to transform lives, solve dilemmas in people's lives, give answers and solutions to people's problems, transform societies and nations for better and to help other people fulfil their own Callings and enter their own Destiny.

God adds days to your life for the sake of those who need you and not for your own sake, meaning that as long as your Calling stops being a gift or a blessing to people then, God has no obligation to adding days to your life.

So, the gift within you called Calling must be treated with respect as valuable.

Sometimes we may knowingly or unknowingly divert our Callings away from being a gift and benefit for others into only benefiting ourselves which will be a tragic and fatal mistake.

3. YOUR CALLING WILL PRESERVE YOU

As stated earlier, your Calling is the what you were born to do and therefore as long as you are fulfilling that Calling then it is incumbent that you remain alive and well. Your Calling is greater than death. God will often protect and preserve us from affliction, sickness and disease and even deliver us from addictions, self-destruction, so that we can fulfil our Purpose and Call.

Without knowing and fulfilling your Calling makes you redundant and irrelevant in a society and nation. So, there are situations where you may suffer and remain unfulfilled if you fail to discover and fulfil your Calling. This means that there are people, societies and nations awaiting for you to discover and fulfil your Calling.

Your disobedience in discovering and fulfilling your Calling means that you are taking up valuable space doing nothing worthwhile in a society and nation. Fulfilling your Calling brings you alive and resurrects anything that was dead within you and it will keep the gifts, talents and skills within you vibrant and operational. So, fulfilling your Calling is the life juice that will usher you to your Destiny.

Queen Esther was indeed a gift to her people when she fulfilled her call in protecting them from being annihilated.

God protects and preserves us because He has a Purpose and Call for us to fulfil. He wants to bring us to a place of usefulness, a place of Purpose and Destiny. So, every time God has delivered you from destruction it has been so that you fulfil your Purpose and Call.

God's Purpose and Call in our life cannot be thwarted by any hand of man or evil

Job 42:2 – *"I know that You can do everything, And that no Purpose of Yours can be withheld from You."*

No matter how much people or the enemy may try to derail you, God has power to ultimately accomplish His plans in our lives as long as we remain obedient and aligned to His plan and agenda.

4. YOUR CALLING HAS A PROCESS

You will not fully discover your Purpose and Calling overnight, nor will you fulfil it overnight, it will require a process and a journey because your Calling unfolds over time and you will continue discovering aspects of it as you go along.

So, it will require you to seek and search deliberately and intentionally relying on the assistance of others like mentors, coaches, and basically the Destiny helpers placed in your life.

Fulfilling your Calling will require you to be equipped in terms of the right character, the right attitudes and mind-set, pure healthy emotions, perceptions, paradigms, motives and agendas, which also involves sharpening and harnessing your gifts and skills.

It will be a process of receiving revelation daily about your Calling and undergoing a daily personal transformation to make you equipped for it, through various painful tests, trials, purging and pruning that will mould and sculpture you emotionally, mentally and spiritually.

5. YOUR CALLING HAS A PLACE

Your Calling must be fulfilled in a particular ordained place or sphere and in an environment and atmosphere where you'll find your people namely those intended to benefit from your Calling. At the place of your Calling, you will find all the resources you will need to fulfil your Calling.

At your place of Assignment, you will encounter several issues such as a culture, traditions, protocols and etiquettes which you will need to adopt and align with or wisely avoid the negative ones. You will also find giants to slay, mountains to command, an old guard to replace, battles to fight, destiny helpers and destiny killers.

Knowing your Place of Assignment and the issues you will encounter there, will greatly prepare you in positioning yourself correctly and handling each issue appropriately.

Your ordained place of assignment will be your thriving ground, where your gifts, skills and strength will operate at their best. It will be a place of power as you make your impact and influence it positively.

6. YOUR CALLING HAS SEASONS

In the course of discovering and fulfilling your Calling you and your Calling will undergo cycles of seasons, that are intended to further empower and equip you and cause your Calling to evolve, expand to wider jurisdictions and have a deeper impact.

There will be seasons of intense criticism and attack by those who are opposed to it. There will be seasons of sowing into your Calling without seeing any fruit. There will also be seasons of preparation in order to lay the proper foundations. Seasons for submitting your Calling for scrutiny vetting and endorsement under a right authority who will help you keep in line and streamline it where necessary.

There will be seasons when your Calling is seemingly irrelevant where even though it is definitely accomplishing its mandate and it is on course. Where it does not receive any public recognition or endorsements, and it may appear like it is not having the necessary impact.

You and your Calling will undergo seasons of waiting and barrenness when there is no evidence of fruit as you wait for certain things to happen or fall into place. Seasons of being hidden in isolation because it is still in its infant stage to protect it from defilement and death.

You must embrace each season and allow each season to do its work on you and your Calling, and ensure you reap from the valuable lessons each season will teach you.

7. **YOUR CALLING WILL COST YOU**

"Focus on the Purpose not the Pain." **Tony Evans**

For you to effectively fulfil your Calling there will definitely be losses and sacrifices along the way in terms of: -

a. **Your Relationships** – not everyone will understand you and your Calling and you may have to say goodbye to some relationships who have no revelation about your Calling.

b. **Your Family** – Closely related to relationships are family members who may also have no revelation about your Calling and may become a hindrance along the way. While you cannot remove these people from your life permanently, you must strategically distance yourself and avoid revealing the details of your Calling to them while you wisely continue to fulfil it.

c. **Materially** – There are some material and physical things, comforts and luxuries etc. that you will need to set aside and give up in order to fulfil your Calling.

d. **Socially** – You will have to give up certain social activities and amenities in order to focus totally on your Calling.

e. **Pain** and reputational risks, you will suffer vicious and severe personal criticism from those who are opposed to your Calling (even false accusations and persecutions etc.)

f. **Personal Loss** - where fulfilling your Calling may cause you to lose certain things you hold dear and valuable, such as positions of power and influence, your status in society, business opportunities etc. Your Calling may conflict with those things.

Irrespective of whatever cost you have to pay, remember that it is worth it as you see the positive impact your Calling is having on mankind and on your society and generation.

Knowing that there is a price to pay, a pain to endure and sacrifices to make will help you to be well prepared and enable you to manage your expectations as you embark on fulfilling your Calling and Destiny.

You Must be able to boldly declare;

My Purpose outweighs my pain

My Destiny outweighs my history

My crown outweighs my cross

My hope outweighs my hardships

God's grace outweighs my shame

The blessing outweighs the burden

God's favour outweighs the frustrations

"Hardships often prepare ordinary people for an extraordinary Destiny." **C.S Lewis**

Destiny Questions to Ponder On

1. *Do you believe that you are devoting sufficient time and energy to fulfilling your Calling?*

2. *Do you think people around you consider your Calling a gift to them, how do you know?*

3. *In what situations has God protected and preserved you because of your Calling?*

4. *What incidents in your life made you realize that your Calling entails a process?*

5. *Have you located the place where you are supposed to fulfil your Calling.*

6. *Which season do you believe to be the most challenging while fulfilling your Calling?*

7. *What price do you believe you have paid so far in fulfilling your Calling?*

This Page Was Intentionally Left Blank

Chapter Four

The Tools of a True Visionary

Accessing The Resources Within And Around You

Chapter Preview

62

1) *Provision for your vision*

2) *Competence and Skills*

3) *Dynamic Associations*

4) *Talents and Gifts*

5) *A Prayer Pattern*

6) *A Strategic Plan*

7) *A Radical Faith*

OPENING REMARKS

Once you have discovered your Calling and you are ready to embark on fulfilling it, there are some tools that you will need in order to fulfil it successfully and effectively.

Tools are essential resources you need to carry out particular functions.

Any tools you need for fulfilling your Destiny, are all available and at your disposal and all you need to do is seek wisdom. Your eyes will be opened and you will become alert and sensitive as to what is around and within you (or within your reach).

Some of the tools you will need are provision for your Vision, competence including skills, expertise and specialized knowledge in the area of your Calling, the relevant relationships and networks, talents and gifts that are already within you, strategic plans, a radical faith and of course prayer.

1. PROVISION FOR YOUR VISION

When you have a true Vision, then you will have the provision.

He who created you and gave you the Calling (that you will fulfil) has the provision that you need to fulfil that Calling. That provision will include relationships, opportunities, material substance (or the knowledge to create it)

The provision available for your life will be according to the Vision for your life.

However, remember that just because He who ordered it will pay for, it does not mean that the provision will come automatically and immediately.

There will be seasons of testing your understanding as to what you need and how to use it, before it can be released to you. There will also be seasons of testing you as to how you value, manage, and steward that provision.

If your Vision is true and aligns with your Destiny, it will most definitely be beyond your ability and beyond your own resources but provision will surely become available.

Finally, you will also be tested in your ability to discern and see the provision and substance already within and around you and how to access it.

You should also know that your generosity and willingness to give is a fundamental trait of a Woman of Destiny. So even as you are assured of provision in fulfilling your Calling, many will be watching to see how generous you are in the giving of yourself and your substance to the work of God, to the needy, to your family, to your society and to your nation.

To that extent your generosity is also a tool in your hands that will attract the provision you need for your Vision.

Once you have made a decision for your Vision the provision will become available.

The very essence of a Woman of Destiny is that she is equipped to nurture and to give life to anything that she touches, so you must constantly ask yourself whether you are giving your most precious resources to your most prized priorities (like the Woman with the alabaster jar) because no one but you knows the cost of the oil in your alabaster box (**Luke 7**).

Your Vision and the provision you need are tied together.

The provision for your Vision will often come when you

embrace and submit to that Vision and you are positioned at the right place of Purpose where you have been ordained.

Remaining obedient and faithful in the fulfilling of your Vision despite the hard times and also being patient. Remaining positive in your attitude without murmuring or complaining and ensuring to have the right agendas and pure motives towards your Calling will guarantee you the provision you need.

When you align yourself with your Vision then the provision will also align itself with your Vision.

2. COMPETENCE AND SKILLS

"The test of true competence is the end results." **L. Ron Hubbard**

This is the ability to do something successfully or efficiently or capability and ability, capacity and proficiency.

"Diligence leads to competence." **Jeffrey Benjamin**

These will include your skills and technical expertise and hard skills. You will need to learn and acquire them and keep sharpening and harnessing them by attending courses and seminars, researching and reading widely to acquire knowledge and information necessary for your Calling.

"Education makes you sufficient, skills make you efficient." ~ **Unknown**

Your skills, knowledge, attributes and abilities must be observable and measurable and must translate to performance.

"Your Calling should be a pointer for your skilled development." **Unknown**

Prayer and a good character alone is not sufficient and even though it will equip and strengthen you, you will also need skills etc. You must proceed to acquire those skills and keep them polished, harnessed and sharpened.

The bridge between your Vision and your greatness is your skills and expertise, and contrary to common belief, your good character on its own is not sufficient to fulfil your Calling. You must combine your character with your competency.

"Strengthen your character and competence and you will enhance your connections and credence." **Unknown**

Many have a Vision and a dream but because they lack the skills and expertise, they remain in a holding position. They become defective vessels for lack of skills, you must prepare for where you are going.

"The future belongs to those who learn more skills and combine them in creative ways." **Robert Greene.**

3. DYNAMIC ASSOCIATIONS

"It is only through the power of association that those with any Calling exercise due influence in their communities." **Elihu Root**

These will include your Destiny provokers, helpers and Destiny connectors who will be part of a wider pool of various relationships, like networks, associations and affiliations that you will definitely require as tools in your journey to Destiny.

"Your network is your net worth." **Porter Gale**

You will need to know how to identify, embrace and appropriately relate to all these various relationships. Furthermore, you will need to know the relevance and value of each relationship, and in which aspect of your Calling they will come in. also the period of time each relationship will be in your life for. While some are long-term, others will be seasonal. You will need to learn the terms of engagement and codes of conduct to apply in each of these relationships for maximum effectiveness.

"Know where you want to go and make sure the right people know about it." **Meredith Mahoney**

You should occupy yourself with people that inspire you, people who provoke you to rise higher and do better. You should not spend your valuable time with people who are not adding to your growth and development or who are not propelling you to your Destiny.

Intentionally surround yourself with dreamers because even though they may have their heads in the clouds they are practical and their feet are firmly on the ground. Such people will help you and push you to realize your own dreams. Remember that people will either inspire you or drain you.

"You are the salt of the earth. But remember that salt is useful when in association but useless in isolation." Israelmore Ayivor

The right associations are those who influence your speech, your thinking and your actions positively towards the fulfilment of your Destiny.

"Too much association with visionless people will blur your Vision until you finally lose sight of your true identity." **Clement Ogedegbe**

Identifying and disconnecting from any wrong relationships that do not propel you to Destiny will be crucial, as well as protecting yourself from those who seek to kill your Destiny.

So, in short, your Calling and Purpose is tied to certain

relationships that you will need to connect to that will empower and propel you to your Destiny. As stated, these are your **Destiny helpers**. However, there will also be relationships that you will need to disconnect from because they will waste your time and deplete your energy and thereby delay you in fulfilling your Destiny namely **Destiny Delayers**. Others will seek to derail, undermine and kill your Destiny, namely your **Destiny killers**. There will be external and internal obstacles and giants that you will need to slay and overcome in order to fulfil your Destiny.

4. TALENTS AND GIFTS

In order to fulfil your Calling, you need tools like the talents and gifts within you. A talent is a natural aptitude of gifts within you. You are already equipped and endowed with the specific talents and gifts that you need to fulfil your Calling and all you need is to release and apply them to their maximum.

Thereafter all you need to do is to keep sharpening and harnessing your talents and gifts the same way you would harness your skills and competence.

"Anyone who develops his gifts and talents will become a commodity." **Myles Munroe**

These gifts and talents are human abilities imparted upon you by God (the author of your Destiny) specifically to endow you and equip you for the fulfilment of your Calling and Destiny. These include spiritual gifts like wisdom, discernment, faith, prophecy. Talents such as public speaking, writing, networking, decision making, critical thinking, entrepreneurship, music etc.

"A winner is one who recognizes his God-given talents, works his tail off to develop them into skills and uses these skills to accomplish his goals." **Larry Bird**

5. PRAYER

"Prayer is man's greatest power." **W. Clement Stone**

Prayer is one of the most powerful **tools** in helping you to fulfil your Calling. In prayer you will get clarity, empowerment, insight and revelation that you would not ordinarily get from any other source. Prayer connects you to God the one who knows the Calling he created you for and you get a better understanding of exactly what you are supposed to be doing whenever you are stuck.

As stated earlier, God is the author of your Calling and Destiny. It will not be possible for you to fulfil that Calling without immersing yourself in God's word from where you will get valuable insight, revelations and divine strategies, directions and instructions. So, you will need to have a disciplined prayer life and walk, spending quality time in the place of prayer in order to receive empowerment, encouragement and to reinforce the anointing already within you for your Calling.

It is in your place of prayer that you will receive downloads from the throne room of heaven regarding every aspect of your Calling and Destiny. It is in the place of prayer that you will know how to use all the other tools available to you.

"Prayer is the nearest approach to God." **William Law**

6. A STRATEGIC PLAN

"There is a strategy for every situation in your life, for every struggle in your life, for every relationship in your life, for every child you are raising, for every job you are after, for every career you want… there is a strategy. There is a God given divine strategy that will bring every obstacle and every crisis in your life down to its knees. All you need to do is pray your way into that strategy." **T.D. Jakes**

Strategy is an approach or tactic, a plan of action, a game plan or a blueprint that you would device in order to fulfil your Calling, by setting strategic goals and prioritizing how you will fulfil them. It is a tool that will guide you step by step in fulfilling your Calling.

You will need to strategize, unpack and set out structures and systems to address the bigger goal. For example; you will need to have a Vision or several Visions and missions which are components of your Calling and which you will need to execute or implement towards the fulfilment of your Calling (together with a well-structured and articulated mission as to how you will implement and execute your Vision and dream).

In addition, you will need to set goals and embark on fulfilling them within a structured timeline and framework. Just like for any project you would need a blueprint, so too for your Calling, you will need a blue print.

7. RADICAL FAITH

Faith is another powerful tool for fulfilling your Call and Destiny. The process of fulfilling your Calling will be faced with a lot of obstacles and hindrances, attacks and challenges, so you must develop a radical faith in God every step of the way. Faith is the ability to hope and trust in things you cannot visibly see but believing that somehow everything and everyone you need will become available.

Faith is also rising above what the circumstances show you and putting your hope and trust into what you know God has told you about you and your Calling.

A radical faith is an insane trust and assurance that what God has promised is true despite every circumstance and reality that is telling you otherwise. Keeping this faith against all the odds is what makes you a Destiny hero.

Faith is seeing light with your heart when your eyes are only seeing darkness.

Destiny Questions to Ponder On

1. *How difficult has it been to get the provision for your Calling, what difficulties have you experienced?*

2. *What competence for your Calling do you find you lack most and how do you think you can go about acquiring it?*

3. *Are there relationships that you might have overlooked and neglected or lost that looking back now you know they were intended for your Calling and if so, what impact did their absence have?*

4. *What gifts and talents within you might you have neglected to unleash or harness and sharpen that are delaying the fulfilment of your Calling?*

5. *How big a role does the tool of Prayer play in fulfilling your Calling?*

6. *What factors do you consider most fundamental in coming up with a strategic plan regarding your Calling?*

7. *In what situations have you encountered a faith failure in fulfilling your Calling so far?*

Chapter Five

The Steps to Birthing Your Visions to Destiny

Understanding The Conceiving And The Carrying Of Your Destiny Pregnancy

Chapter Preview

1. *Breaking Your Barrenness*

2. *Conceiving the Seed of Your Vision*

3. *Carrying the pregnancy of Your Vision*

4. *Enduring Your Labour Pains*

5. *Pushing Out your Vision*

6. *The Cutting of the Cord of your Vision*

7. *The Crying Out of your Vision*

OPENING REMARKS

The terms Vision, Assignment, Purpose, Calling and Destiny are all interrelated and we usually use them interchangeably because they ultimately relate to the same thing. The term Vision used here relates to the objectives and goals that are part of your Calling. The aspects of the Calling that you are fulfilling comprising of the assignments and tasks.

In order to birth your Vision (without aborting or miscarrying it, and without having a still birth or birthing a deformed Vision) there are certain steps to follow.

These steps of birthing your Vision are similar symbolically to the steps of birthing a natural baby. So as a Woman who has birthed a child and even for those who have not, these steps will resonate very clearly.

The steps towards birthing your Vision and the steps after you Birth that Vision are extremely crucial in ensuring your effectiveness and success. They include; breaking your barrenness that will then enable you to conceive that Vision and go on to carry it through its full term to the point of labouring, pushing and birthing it out.

1. BREAKING YOUR BARRENNESS

As a Woman of Destiny, you will have a revelation that there is a that you were created to fulfil. Yet you may come to a point where you know that you have not yet conceived and birthed that Calling and Purpose and hence the reason you may be experiencing a non-fulfilled life and restlessness. This means that you are in a dry and barren season whereby that barrenness needs to be broken and that dry season needs to come to an end so that you can conceive and bring forth your Calling.

In order to eventually birth your Vision and Calling you must first conceive it and in order to conceive it you must first have your barrenness broken which will entail three steps as follows:

i. **Firstly**, a **healthy 'womb'** symbolizing your ability to conceive the seed of Destiny (which is a seed of greatness). A conducive, healthy womb in this context symbolizes a right fertile and positive mind-set and attitude as well as healthy emotions and a healthy lifestyle.

When preparing your physical womb for a physical baby, the doctor will scan for any cysts, fibroids or any abnormalities etc. Likewise, symbolically when preparing to birth a Vision and Calling, your heart condition, emotions, mind-sets, attitudes etc. need scanning to ensure there is no mental and emotional unwellness (that there are no hindrances, such as a negative mind-set or toxic emotions, past pain, woundedness, anger, offense, hardness of heart, bitterness, wrong paradigms and perceptions, doubts, fears, unforgiving etc.) which could stand in the way of a successful conception. So, you must constantly off load every such toxic baggage.

This means that in order for you to conceive your Vision and Calling it is important to ensure that you are walking right spiritually, emotionally, mentally, financially and generally with regard to all areas of your lifestyle so that you start on the right foundation (lest you conceive, carry and birth your Vision and Calling from an unhealthy 'womb').

This is similar with a physical baby where the doctor ensures that your womb is healthy (by removing any sicknesses within it) before advising you to proceed with the conception, (lest your baby be conceived, carried and birthed from an unhealthy womb).

ii.   Secondly, **intimate relationship –** in a natural marriage there needs to be intimacy between a couple for them to conceive a physical baby, and just like when preparing for that physical baby. Likewise, and symbolically, you will need to have, develop and maintain a healthy intimate relationship and walk with God because He is the one who will impart you with that seed for your Vision and Calling (whereby you know and hear His voice, read and meditate on His word, obey and walk in accordance with His commands and communicate with Him in your place of prayer).

In addition, God will feed you with his word, insights and revelation to fortify you for the seed that He has imparted into you. This is to ensure that like a physical womb your spiritual womb is strong enough to carry the seed of greatness.

iii.   Thirdly, **being naked and open** – in a natural marriage when conceiving a physical baby, you will need to be naked and open in order to be impregnated and you will need to be positioned correctly for that the seed to take root within you.

Likewise, when conceiving your Vision, you will need to be symbolically naked and open before God (whereby there are no hidden agendas or motives). You will need to be honest and lay bare every aspect in your life that is not right before God so that He can deal with everything that He needs to deal with (like toxic emotions, unbelief, negative mind-sets, wrong financial habits, bad stewardship of resources, unhealthy relationships, hardness of heart, doubts etc.)

It means being completely transparent about yourself, your sins, failings, weaknesses, shortcomings etc. agreeing to walk away from them. Being open to God about your apprehensions and fears and not hiding anything whatsoever.

Once you have satisfied the above conditions, then your season of barrenness and waiting, will turn, and your barrenness will be broken.

Whether you are seeking to conceive a physical baby or to conceive your Vision and Calling (chances are that during your season of waiting and barrenness) there will be those who will mock, taunt and ridicule you because of your condition. Instead of wasting your energy responding to them, you should let their mockery provoke you into pursuing the breaker of you barrenness.

There will also be others who may seek to dissuade you against seeking to conceive your seed of Destiny because they do not have the revelation you have regarding your Call and Vision. Their constant pleas with you to stop waiting and instead settle for less, should not upset you. You should ignore them and forge on. Not everyone in your life knows where you are going and what you have been called for, so many will not understand your deep and desperate yearning to conceive and birth it.

2. CONCEIVING THE SEED OF YOUR VISION

Once your barrenness is broken then the next step is to conceive. You will need to position and align yourself strategically to conceive. It will entail identifying and connecting to your impregnator and imparter. Separating yourself and surrendering yourself to receive.

I. Identifying and connecting with your impregnator and imparter.

When conceiving a physical baby, it is important for you to be impregnated by the right person namely your spouse. So, at this point your fidelity and commitment to your relationship with your spouse is crucial. You must avoid straying away from your spouse lest you be impregnated by an imposter and you conceive and birth a baby that does not bare the DNA of your spouse.

Likewise, when conceiving your vision, it is important for you to be imparted by God. So, at this point your faithfulness and commitment in your relationship with God is crucial. You must avoid straying from God lest you conceive and birth an "Ishmael" vision that does not have the hand of God upon it.

II. Separating yourself.

When you are conceiving a physical baby, you must be in private with your spouse behind closed doors and not in public. Likewise, impartation of your Vision and Calling by God must be in private during your seasons of separation from the public crowds. You must immerse yourself in God. It also means cutting yourself away from the noise and many voices and distractions and allowing only one voice (the voice of your imparter and the author of your Destiny). This entails a consecration and a sanctification.

III. Surrendering Yourself To Receive.

During physical conception with your spouse, you must surrender yourself completely and utterly to your impregnator (without resisting). Be still and trust the one impregnating you and be extremely receptive.

Likewise, as God is beginning to impart you with the seed of Destiny, you must adopt an attitude of trust, be receptive, yielded and humble. Position yourself in a manner (meaning a right attitude and mind-set and right heart condition) that allows the seed to take root, as opposed to being anxious and unstable lest you interfere with the impartation.

When getting the impartation for your Vision and Calling, it means that you will get a downloading and some measure of understanding of what your conceiving. You may not get the entire complete download because discovering and understanding your Vision and Calling is a process.

Likewise, when you are conceiving and carrying your physical baby you may not yet know whether it is a boy or girl and how it will really look like or its characteristics etc. because those features will evolve through a process of growth.

3. CARRYING THE PREGNANCY OF YOUR VISION

Once you have conceived, you will carry your physical baby or your seed of Destiny through 3 stages namely; the first trimester / season, the second trimester/ season and third trimester/ season before you actually birth it.

i. The First Trimester

With a physical pregnancy, during the **first trimester**, it will not show outwardly. However inwardly you know you are carrying a baby because you will begin to experience certain uncomfortable changes and discomforts like nausea etc.)

Likewise, the Vision is not visible outwardly but all the signs of it being within you will be there. You will start experiencing changes like new responsibilities, roles and obligations. Some will entail a process of learning taking you out of your comfort zone because the Vision you are carrying will make a demand on you.

When carrying a physical baby some physical changes will start taking place in your body like the tenderness of your body etc. which will be uncomfortable and painful.

With regard to your Vision and Calling there will also be a "stretching" which symbolizes that you begin to expand and grow mentally, emotionally and spiritually (in order to accommodate the vision growing within you). The stretching of your mind as you study and research about the Vision you are carrying as well as praying over it may become time consuming and a demand on your energy.

Your physical pregnancy is hidden from the public during this first trimester because it is a delicate time when anything could go wrong. Likewise, your vision is still hidden from the public during this early season and it is normally wise to keep it that way, to avoid your Destiny killers from interfering with it. So, no matter how excited you are, you must resist every temptation to reveal or show off about what you are carrying to the wrong people, (whether it be your physical baby or your Vision and Calling that you are carrying).

With a physical pregnancy some of the dangers of this first trimester are a miscarriage at the early stages. Your womb may reject the baby, because either there is some sickness in the womb such as cysts, fibroids etc. which had not been removed. If they had been removed then for whatever reason they have grown back again after you have conceived and they become a danger to the baby. The miscarriage could also happen as a result of some other causes.

Likewise with regards to your Vision and Calling it is possible to go through an abortion of Purpose (whereby some of the issues like toxic emotions and negative mind-sets had never been removed from your 'womb'). If they had then they have come back to defile your 'womb' after your impartation with the vision and hence the abortion of Purpose.

The reason both the physical baby and the vision undergo a miscarriage or an abortion of Purpose is because if they were to continue growing under those circumstances then inevitably the physical baby will grow up with serious defects that would hinder the growth and development. The vision would grow into a defective Vision whose growth and development would be greatly prejudiced as it would be based on a wrong foundation.

If fortunately, a physical baby does not undergo a miscarriage, then at this stage you must start eating right and taking the right vitamins to fortify your body and baby so that you birth a healthy one.

Likewise, and symbolically and if fortunately, your vision does not result in an abortion of Purpose, then you will need to start feeding and taking in a healthy dose of what is pure, true and positive, wise counsel and right relationships to ensure your vision gets fortified so that you bring forth a strong Calling.

Your physical pregnancy trimesters (when your carrying your baby) and your times of carrying your vision are seasons of expectancy. You must maintain a positive attitude of expectation. You must speak to your baby or the Vision as it grows within you by feeding it and empowering it with words of affirmation etc.

ii. The Second Trimester

During this **second trimester** your physical pregnancy is now visible to the public. Your clothes and garments will need to change to avoid suffocating what you are carrying. Your eating habits will change so that you eat the right foods that are healthy and nutritious and that will enhance the healthy growth of your baby.

With regard to your Vision and Calling during this second trimester your feeding habits will need to upgrade. You will need to take extra care with regard to what materials you read, what you listen to, and what you partake in (in terms of friendships, social activities etc.) Any wrong feeding will defile the vision you are carrying whether it is a physical baby or a Vision.

With a physical pregnancy, in this trimester you will need to lower the height of your shoe heels lest you trip and fall and injure your physical baby.

With regard to your Vision during this season you will also lower your 'footwear' symbolizing humbling yourself by dealing with pride. So, you will begin to wear 'lower heels' which symbolizes adopting an attitude of **teachability** to avoid tripping and falling which could damage the reputation of the vision within you.

At this stage you will need advice from those mothers who have given birth to babies before as well as the help of a midwife and doctors. With regard to your Vision, you will need the advice of those who have been there before you, like Destiny helpers, mentors, coaches, Destiny connectors etc.

The greatest danger in this trimester/season is a spirit of pride because your Vision is now showing and it is beautiful and admirable. You must guard against such pride because your

Vision is yet to be fully birthed and these are just signs of its potential. You should seek wise counsel and learn as much as you can about this process and season.

Maintaining a right attitude without murmuring and complaining about the hard process, the discomfort and the painful stretching is important. Embrace the process and choose to respond with gratitude and endurance. The pain and discomfort is surely worth it.

iii. The Third Trimester

The next and final trimester of carrying your physical baby is where you have been expanded and stretched to full capacity and the discomfort and pain is greater. Your ability to move around is slowed and you need more help than ever in handling yourself and what you are carrying.

At this stage your garments, and clothes are so tight that you are extremely uncomfortable and you result to the loosest and most comfortable clothing and footwear because sometimes your feet could also be swollen and painful.

With regard to your Vision during this final season, your mental and emotional capacity have grown. You have matured and have a deeper revelation of the significance of what you are carrying. The responsibility and weight of the greatness you are carrying is upon you heavily, and you need a lot of help from the right people.

Your family and friends make it quite clear that the baby you are about to birth is not for you alone and that there will also own and enjoy that baby.

Likewise, the joyful reaction of your loved ones makes you know that the Vision you are carrying is not about you, but it is about many others and that it is intended to impact and positively influence many. So, you become more careful and responsible in guarding it.

At this stage you must die to your flesh and selfish indulgences your ego, your plans, your timing, your own way, your need to be in control and your need to be right and instead simply surrender to the process and endure.

4. ENDURING YOUR LABOUR PAINS

This is a crucial step in birthing your baby and probably the most challenging step. It's during this stage that most women are not sure they actually want to birth their baby because of the intense labour pains caused by the contractions as the baby tries to squeeze out of the birth canal.

The labour pains when you are birthing a physical baby are so excruciating. You need the help of the doctor and midwife to help you manage this pain and to coach you how to breath so that the pain becomes bearable.

With regard to your Vision this is a season of painful effort, determination, hard work and action that is costly, inconvenient and uncomfortable as you prepare to birth your Vision. Your capacities and abilities will be stretched to breaking point as your vision, now quite developed begins to get ready to manifest.

This is the stage when you undergo the fiercest storms, harshest trials and tribulations, persecutions, self-doubt and fear because the enemy of your Destiny is fighting to hinder you from actually manifesting your Vision and Call.

It is often at the eve of your greatest breakthrough that you will encounter your deepest challenges and endure your deepest pain and experience your highest doubts, thereby making you almost quit and threatening to abort your Vision.

It is at this stage you will need your midwife symbolizing your Destiny helpers (mentors, or spiritual authority). They will help you birth your Vision by guiding you on how to be positioned, and how to have the right attitude, how to endure the pain and how to push out your Vision.

Your labour will entail three things namely, enduring the pain, guarding the atmosphere and the environment in the birthing room and proper positioning.

i. When birthing a physical baby, you will be stretched beyond reasonable limits and beyond what you think you can bear in order to allow your baby to come out. Your Vision is always bigger than you and that's the reason you must be stretched to the extreme maximum emotionally, mentally etc. as you undergo those challenges that come on the eve of your breakthrough.

No matter how much you think the stretching will destroy you (whether you are birthing a physical baby or your Vision) it is actually very well measured and physically it will not kill you or your baby and symbolically it will not kill you or your Vision.

During a physical labour for a physical baby, your labouring stage will be physically and excruciatingly painful. As your baby is seeking to come out, it will be accompanied by very agonizing spasms and you will reach a point where you sincerely believe that the pain will kill you.

Likewise, during the birthing of your Vision, the trials and tribulations will be more painful and intense as you symbolically labour to bring it forth. The more painful your labour is, the more powerful the Vision you are bringing forth.

Just like labour pains will be more painful where a physical baby is bigger and weighs more.

ii. The physical place where you birth your physical baby must be very clean, very hygienic and warm enough with all the right equipment and the right and experienced people to handle your baby as you birth it, such as breathing machines, incubators etc.

A wrong atmosphere and environment can seriously harm your physical baby and cause contamination, diseases and infirmities that will compromise the health and growth of your baby.

Likewise, and symbolically the place and environment where you birth your Vision, must be morally and spiritually clean. Surrounded by the right doctrine and teachings, right mind-sets, pure emotions plus with the right resources, healthy relationships, gifts, talents and skills to receive and handle your Vision as you birth it (such as your Destiny helpers and the specific Destiny midwife in your life).

iii. When birthing a physical baby, it is important that it be positioned correctly with its head facing down towards the birth canal not facing the opposite way. If your doctor and midwife do not detect this on time (so as to turn the baby around using their expertise hand techniques) then this could result in a breech birth which can sometimes compromise the safety of the baby.

Likewise, a wrong positioning can harm your Vision and lay the weak and wrong foundations that will not be able to hold and sustain that Vision later on during challenges and attacks.

Sometimes when you make the mistake of de-positioning yourself from your place of Purpose (which is also your place of birthing), that Vision which you are carrying becomes wrongly positioned. It becomes difficult and dangerous to bring it forth. Only a good Destiny midwife can help in rectifying that position by counselling you to return to your right place of Purpose in order to birth your Vision at the right place.

5. PUSHING OUT YOUR VISION

Remember that no matter how excruciating your labour pains may be, they will always bear fruit. Do not be distracted by the pain, instead you should focus on the push which symbolizes travailing in prayer and intercession.

The stage finally comes when you must push out your physical baby. This is the stage where you must exert yourself most and use all your energy and strength in order to push out that baby. Birthing is not automatic and it requires your great effort and focused concentration and participation which shows your passion and your desire to have this baby no matter how painful it is.

It is at this stage that your doctor and midwife, and even your spouse will be most useful in encouraging you. Holding your hand and cheering you on not to give up. More importantly to coach you on how to push and open up so that you do not hinder and suffocate the baby from coming out. You have come this far and you might as well finish the job.

Likewise, you come to the step and stage where your Vision is ready to manifest and you must apply yourself diligently, deliberately, and intentionally.

Be totally focused in listening to and obeying every instruction of your Destiny midwife as to what you need to do in order to successfully and safely bring forth the Vision you have been carrying.

You may lose the strength to push because you have become exhausted (especially where the labour period is extended) and this could endanger the baby and suffocate it because failure to push is hindering it from coming out for air.

Birthing your Vision and Calling can also be hindered by lack of strength to push enough where you lose faith on the eve of delivering your Vision and Calling. You have come from so far carrying such a heavy Vision and going through all manner of trials and tribulations. At this point when you are just about to bring forth you may unfortunately become too weary because of having been strong for so long. That is where your Destiny midwife comes in because they speak strength and encouragement to you reminding you that the end is near and that you must not give up.

The other factor is where the labour period takes too long and this time it is your baby that gets tired of the process and this can result in foetal distress where the baby dies before coming out.

Another factor that could hinder and interfere with a successful birth is where the baby size and weight is too big for the birth canal and it is unable to fit through. If your doctor and midwife do not make a quick decision to give you a caesarean section then your baby can be endangered and result in a still birth.

Also, the Vision you are carrying may be too great for you to bring forth alone and that's why you need Destiny helpers around you.

The 'birth canal' from where your Vision is coming out, which symbolizes your "faith channel", may be too small and narrow because of your fears and anxieties as to whether you are capable of bringing forth this great Vision. This then leads to delay and procrastination in giving birth and your Vision could die or get crippled by the delay in birthing it.

Or maybe you may procrastinate in birthing your Vision sometimes out of fear or doubt. By being too lazy to apply yourself thereby suffocating and killing your Vision inside you because you failed to bring it forth at the due time and season.

This is an instrument like tongs that encircle a baby's head and assist in birthing it out where it is taking too long for the baby to come out either because the mother is too tired to push or the baby is also too tired to respond to the pushing and to avoid foetal distress, the doctor must use forceps.

During this stage of birthing, the doctor must be extremely careful not to damage the baby's head in the process of using the forceps, which could result in brain damage etc.

Likewise, when birthing your Vision, your Destiny midwives, mentors and Destiny helpers must be very careful to pray the right prayers speak the right words, declare and decree the right declarations, over your Vision because any idle word over your Vision by your helpers could cause irrevocable damage. So, in this context of birthing your Vision, the "forceps" symbolize the prayers, words, decrees and declarations used in helping to birth your Vision because they help to push out your Vision when you have become too tired to push it out yourself.

The place of Purpose could signify either your church, family, business enterprise, institution, organization, society or nation. There is where you are supposed to be located and where you are supposed to birth your Vision and fulfil your Calling. So, when you deposition yourself just before birthing and you come out of that right place where you are supposed to be and go to a wrong place. This will compromise the safety of the Vision you are birthing.

Just like you had to be naked and open to conceive, you also have to be naked and open to bring it forth. With the birthing of a physical baby, you have to remove any clothing blocking the birth gate. When birthing your Vision, the nakedness and openness symbolizes removing any hindrances whatsoever that may hinder the birthing of your Vision.

Just like a physical baby cannot be birthed when you are fully clothed so too you need to be completely naked honest and open when birthing your Vision (without any hidden agendas), so that your heart, emotions, mind-sets and motives must be pure as regards the Vision that you are birthing. For example, by knowing that your Vision is not about you, or about your selfish ambitions, but for the welfare of others, your society and nation.

When birthing a physical baby perhaps the greatest danger comes at the pushing stage, where you have to be extremely attentive to the instructions of your doctor and midwife, (so that you do not either push too early or too late). Pushing too early will damage the baby and pushing too late will cause foetal distress, resulting in a still birth.

So, listening and obeying the instructions of your doctor and midwife is very important and you cannot afford to ignore those instructions or seek to take matters in your own hands and decide to birth your own way.

Likewise, when you are birthing your Vision, there is sometimes a temptation to go ahead of the right timing and ignore the instructions of your Destiny midwife, mentors and other Destiny helpers. This will threaten the welfare of your Vision and expose it too soon and risk defilement and attacks from the enemies of your Vision.

Perhaps worse than your failure to listen and obey the instructions of your Destiny midwife, is to listen to the wrong voices and wrong instructions of your enemies who will mislead you and deceive you during this very crucial stage. You will end up killing your Vision because of wrong relationships, wrong voices and wrong instructions.

You must be careful to discern to connect to the right Destiny midwife and Destiny helpers who will not kill your Vision when helping you to bring it forth. Also remember that the enemy of your Destiny prowls around in your birthing room (meaning your place of Purpose) waiting to destroy your Vision when it comes out, so you need serious prayer warriors and intercessors waging a warfare on your behalf which is what good Destiny midwives and Destiny helpers do.

6. THE CUTTING OF THE CORD OF YOUR VISION

There is an umbilical cord that connects a physical baby and the mother while in the womb which is essential for the feeding, nurturing and sustenance of the baby while in the womb.

Likewise, there is a symbolic cord that connects you to your vision while you are carrying it which must be symbolically cut at the time of birthing. The cutting of the cord entails a separating, a releasing and a receiving.

Just after a physical baby is birthed and before it encounters the outside world, there is a cutting of the umbilical cord (which was connecting that physical baby with his mother) in order for the baby to come out and become a separate individual from the mother.

Likewise, when you have birthed your Vision, your emotional connection with that Vision and your selfish ownership of it has to be cut. So that others can also receive that Vision and run with it as they help you to fulfil it.

Therefore, there is the cutting and separation of the umbilical cord which is no longer necessary for a physical baby because the baby can now feed directly through its own mouth (as opposed to when it was being fed through the mother feeding herself and the food would reach the baby through the umbilical cord).

Likewise with your Vision, it is also the separation of any "ties and hold" you may have on that Vision you have birthed that may cause you to own it selfishly for your own selfish agendas (and to refuse the input of others or the benefit to others).

Afterwards the physical baby is released to and received by others who also own the baby like the father, siblings, relatives etc. Those who will also be involved in that baby going forward. Likewise, when you birth your vision, you must release it to be received by those who were intended to benefit from it or to be part of it as well going forward. This is because your Vision is never about you alone or for you alone and it includes other designated people.

7. THE CRYING OUT OF YOUR VISION

Once you birth your baby the first thing it usually does is to cry out and in crying out it takes in the necessary oxygen into its lungs in order to survive. Likewise, when you birth your Vision it "cries out" as it comes into the reality of the real world.

The crying out of your baby or Vision, entails a slapping, an opening up and a cleaning and cleansing.

i) The Slap

Just like a physical baby sometimes has to be sharply slapped to give its first cry and open up its lungs, likewise your Vision needs to be given a symbolic 'slap' so as to announce its arrival and propel it into the world where it will make impact and transform lives. This "slap" is symbolized by the first radical utterance you or your Destiny midwife, Destiny Helpers etc. make about your Vision once you birth it, which may often be a painful sharp rebuke like this quote from an unknown source, "This Vision is not about you. History will judge you if you mishandle it" **or something equally sharp.**

ii) The Opening Up

It is important in the case of a physical baby that it makes its first cry to open up its lungs and allow oxygen in. Likewise, your Vision will need to make an audible noise and acclamation that it has arrived. This sometimes is in the form of a clear announcement of its arrival in the presence of the targeted beneficiaries, vision helpers who will help you fulfil that Vision going forward.

iii) The Cleaning and Cleansing

Just like a physical baby is birthed and covered with amniotic fluid which was covering it and protecting it in the mother's womb and which must be cleaned after it is birthed. Likewise, when you birth your Vision, it will need to be "cleaned" in order to remove any undue and unhealthy emotional attachment from you so that your Vision can be embraced by others, and be for others not just for yourself.

Destiny Questions to Ponder On

1. Which area or areas in your life have you experienced the longest barrenness?

2. What signs made you realize that you had conceived whatever you had been barren for?

3. What stage of your "pregnancy" do you find most challenging?

4. What in your view is the greatest threat or danger in your labouring stage?

5. What should be the greatest motivation for you when pushing out your Vision?

6. What aspect of the de-cording do you find most fundamental and why?

7. Do you think that your Vision can live to fulfilment even without a crying out?

This Page Was Intentionally Left Blank

Chapter Six

The Steps After Birthing Your Visions to Destiny

Safeguarding The Vision After Birthing It

Chapter Preview

1. *The Naming*

2. *The Weaning*

3. *The immunization*

4. *The Empowering*

5. *The Branding*

6. *The Threshing, Purging and Pruning*

7. *The Releasing*

OPENING REMARKS

After birthing your Vision successfully, there are several steps and actions that you need to take to ensure that your Vision does not die after birthing or become defiled or crippled.

Unfortunately, sometimes after you birth a physical baby it may undergo what is called a cot death for whatever reason. Likewise, your Vision may experience a 'cot death' after you birth it for whatever reasons.

The following steps and actions are similar and symbolic of those you would take after birthing a physical baby, like the naming, the weaning, the immunizing, the empowering, nurturing or educating, the branding, the disciplining or the threshing out of undesirables, and the releasing for that baby to benefit others.

1. THE NAMING

The power in a name will propel someone or something in a particular direction.

The name you give your physical baby may influence the life of that baby positively or negatively, depending on the meaning of that name and what it represents. For example, some names given to some babies have such negative connotations which influence the babies personality and character negatively.

Whereas when a baby is given a positive and Destiny oriented name, chances are the power in that name will propel that child in the right direction and will help to define that child positively. When a baby is born it is given a name that gives it identity otherwise it will be identityless.

A nameless Vision is powerless and identity less. You must name your Vision because there is power in a name and whatever name you give it, will define it. Your Vision will also manifest itself within the confines of the name you give it. The name also lets others know the intended impact that the Vision will have.

There is power in a name because it gives your Vision a clear identity and mandate. The name you give it speaks to the use and direction and the course it will take, because it will align with its name.

It is crucial for the name of your Vision to be correct from the beginning and NOT contrary what your Vision is about and where your Vision needs to go.

The name you give your baby or Vision will make or break it hence the importance of correct naming for correct identity.

2. THE WEANING

At some point with your physical baby you must wean it by graduating it from what you initially fed it with to feeding it with tougher substance in order to strengthen it. To enable it to start standing on its own feet. So, the baby will move from feeding on milk to solid foods as it grows.

In fact, during each birthday of your baby you will notice that your baby will require new, bigger clothes and shoes. As it grows it will continue to grow out of the smaller ones.

For your Vision, it could mean injecting more resources, deeper and higher programs, wider reach and jurisdiction or more sophisticated structures and systems as it expands and grows. This means that at every annual anniversary of your Vision, it will require a new "ephod" as it outgrows the previous one.

"Ephod" symbolizes new dreams and goals, new strategies so that your Vision will have more influence and impact, productivity and fruitfulness at each anniversary.

You will have some understanding (though not a complete understanding) of the reason for your Vision as you conceive it (in terms of what it was intended to accomplish so that you can then release it to do so).

In fact, often, some of the prerequisites to conceiving your Vision is knowing somehow what and why that Vision is intended to do. So that where your reasons for wanting to conceive and birth it are selfish then the conception of it may be delayed until you have come to a revelation that your Vision is not about you (but also for the benefit of others). Hence the reason you must wean it and ultimately release it to bless others.

3. THE IMMUNIZATION

Immunization is a form of protection or exemption by putting an immunity against something harmful so as to make that which you are protecting resistant to that harm. It is usual for a physical baby to undergo various immunizations especially during the first months of its life to protect it from all manner of sicknesses, diseases and afflictions like polio, measles, cholera, typhoid etc. which would come against it if it was not immunized.

The reason for this immunization is to enable the baby to grow strong into a healthy adult without being hampered by those sicknesses, diseases and afflictions and to enable that child to have a meaningful and Purposeful life.

Immunization of a physical baby may sometimes need to be boosted in order to strengthen the immunity within the baby to fight off any sicknesses, diseases and afflictions.

Just like babies must be immunized from diseases and infections so too you must "immunize" your Vision so as to protect it and build immunity within it against any attacks, criticism, opposition and threats and from being distorted or derailed from what it was intended to accomplish.

"Immunization" for your Vision could entail building in solid systems and structures of accountability and oversight, having a board of advisors and mentors to vet your actions plus checks and balances in place, laying a proper, moral and legal foundation is another way of immunization to prevent your Vision from becoming disqualified or rejected as one which is weak without a proper foundation.

Just like with a physical baby the immunization of your Vision may sometimes need boosting in order to ensure that it remains strong against threats and attacks coming against it.

4. THE EMPOWERING

For a physical baby, **empowering** includes feeding, educating, training, mentoring, disciplining etc. Feeding the baby with the right nutrition and fortifying it with the right vitamins to enable proper growth and development.

Educating means instilling the right information and knowledge that will help the baby to grow up to be productive and fruitful in society and to become a relevant valuable person in the nation. Training means imparting skills and expertise and harnessing those skills and expertise so that the baby grows to be a competent person in their area of vocation. Mentoring means imparting the right morals, values and principles that will enable the baby to grow into a person with good character and integrity and to make the right choices and decisions. Surrounding your baby with the right people and removing the wrong people. While **disciplining** entails correcting, rebuking and guiding that child to grow up in the right ways and in the right path.

Likewise for your Vision, empowering includes feeding (which symbolizes instilling the right goals and strategies so that it may have direction), educating (which symbolizes upgrading it in terms of innovative technologies and systems with new ways of thinking and new ways of doing things), training (which symbolizes implanting the right materials, programs and projects that will benefit the intended target group of that vision), mentoring (which symbolizes imparting the right principles and values into that vision), disciplining (which symbolizes purging anything that has come in to contaminate the vision, sieving and sifting the positive from the negative so as to keep the vision pure, legitimate and authentic, it also means removing any people you had brought into the vision carelessly or emotionally and who are no longer adding value) etc.

Empowering your vision also means sowing into it by investing more resources so that it can be more productive and fruitful in the course of time.

It also means knitting it together with like-minded partners, strategic alliances and collaborations. Empowering it also means subjecting it to regular, SWOT analysis etc. to remove any weak links and enhance its strengths.

5. **THE BRANDING**

This means speaking positive things into and about your physical baby and as it grows into a child and matures into a young adult. Ensuring that you also speak those good things about your child to others so to brand him or her positively and open up opportunities and necessary doors (in either business, career, social circles, and networks etc.) To connect that child to the right relationships that will propel him or her in the right direction where they can thrive, be fruitful and productive.

Learning to speak and impact the right and positive words about your child is also a way of boosting confidence and a healthy self-esteem, self-worth and value into that child which will brand him and propel him in the right direction.

In addition, speaking to your child and to others about the gifts, talents and skills in your child and about the potential within him for the Calling and Destiny he has been called to. This is a way of branding him and letting everyone who matters know the Purpose he was intended for and the Calling he will ultimately fulfil.

So too your Vision needs to be branded so as to adopt the right image and identity and to carry the attractiveness and marketability that it needs to have in order to communicate its value.

The brand identity of your Vision will create a visual identity that becomes the tangible representation of its brand giving it its appeal, essence and promise.

Whenever your Vision hits a snag and maybe gets defiled with a scandal, false accusations, smear campaigns etc. then you must "re-brand" it and clean it up so that it is restored to it right image and credibility. Even where that loss of reputation and credibility was not externally inflicted (but internally inflicted by your own poor choices and poor moral judgments) then you must embark on taking responsibility owning your mistakes and moving on to clean up and rebrand the image of your Vision so that it can continue to fulfil its intended Purpose.

6. THE THRESHING, THE PURGING AND THE PRUNING

As your physical baby grows into a child and young adult (and no matter how well you parent them) they may acquire bad habits and behaviors due to several factors such as the environments they may come into, and the people they may interact with outside of the home. The influences children receive from external sources may cause them to question the values and principles that you have instilled in them. You will need to do some threshing in the way of disciplining so as to separate the good things in them from the bad things without destroying the child or young adult which means that you must have the right methods of disciplining.

This will also entail purging out any habits and behaviours that have become embedded in their mind-sets and in their emotions. Also pruning out undesirables in them that are hindering proper growth and development in the right direction.

Likewise, once your Vision has been in the open for a while it will inevitably attract tares within it that have been planted by the enemies of your Vision (such as smears, wrong perceptions, wrong labelling and stigmas, false identities etc.) A time comes when your Vision has grown but it has such "tares" and "weeds" within it. Threshing it will be the only way to separate the good from the bad so that the real harvest of your Vision can be seen. This threshing will entail removing the wrong people that you had brought into the Vision as helpers who have now become a liability. Disconnecting from wrong relationships, partnerships and alliances that you had connected to that were either not right for your Vision. Even where they were right their motives and agendas have now changed and become harmful for your Vision and you must part ways.

It also means correcting the wrong perceptions by communicating to all those who matter to the Vision and giving them the right information about the Vision (its proper Purpose objectives and goals) so as to remove the wrong perceptions etc.

However, it may be difficult to remove the bad without affecting the good, so you must learn right timing and right methods of weeding out the tares (whether those tares are bad people, partnerships, programs, perceptions, cultures, atmospheres etc.). You must use a lot of wisdom in undertaking this threshing, purging and pruning just the same way that you must use a lot of sensitivity and wisdom when disciplining your young adult or child.

7. THE RELEASING

Finally, a time will come when your baby becomes a child and from a child to a young adult and then become a full-grown adult (who is ready to generate his own income and resources and stand on his own feet and to even marry and have his own family). This means you will have to release them physically and emotionally to live their own lives and make their own decisions and ultimately fulfil their Calling and Destiny.

Your act of releasing them means becoming selfless by realizing that, the person (who was once a baby) was intended to grow up to become a benefit and a blessing to many others in his society, nation next generation (and not only for benefitting you and your small nuclear family).

Likewise, a time will come when your Vision has developed to a place where it begins to fulfil its goals, impact and transform people, societies and nations. It becomes grounded, credible and legitimate enough, for you to release it to benefit those it was intended to benefit and to become a legacy for the next generation.

Releasing your Vision is like sowing it for the benefit of mankind. Your dream or Vision must live and not die so that it can accomplish its Purpose.

Failure to release and entrust your Vision to others may suffocate and relegate it to oblivion. You must understand the seasons and the times and allow others to run with the Vision that you've conceived and birthed so that they take it further, higher and wider than you could have taken it yourself.

Destiny Question To Ponder On

1. *Do you believe that you have named your Vision correctly? Does your Vision answer to its name?*

2. *What challenges might you have encountered in weaning your Vision?*

3. *What defilements and contaminations do you believe that your Vision needed immunization from?*

4. *What other ways have you sought to empower your Vision?*

5. *Are you completely confident that the branding of your Vision is clear to all those it needs to be clear to?*

6. *What other things do you think your Vision requires threshing from and have you sufficiently submitted your Vision for thorough threshing?*

7. *Do you believe that you have sufficiently released your Vision to serve mankind?*

Chapter Seven

Positioned For Influence

Doing The Right Thing At The Right Place

Chapter Preview

1. *Understanding Your Positioning*

2. *Your Positioning Is Tied To Your Purpose*

3. *Locate And Step Into Your Place And Sphere*

4. *Each One Has A Place And A Sphere To Influence*

5. *Beware Of Being Positioned in The Wrong Place And Sphere*

6. *You Will Thrive At Your Right Place And Sphere*

7. *You Are Sent To Impact Your Place And Sphere Positively*

1. UNDERSTANDING YOUR POSITIONING

With regard to Positioning, the basic traditional dictionary definition of "**positioning**" is putting, arranging or placing someone or something in a particular place or way usually for a particular Purpose. Positioning is also a marketing concept commonly used in business to refer to the place that a particular brand occupies in the minds of the intended customers.

"**Positioning**" in our context here, refers to the act of you being placed, planted or settled in a particular specific place or sphere within a society or nation from where you will operate and fulfil your Calling and Destiny.

This is often referred to as your ordained place of Purpose or your place of assignment, your mountain or sector etc. Suffice to say that, it represents or refers to an area of activity, interests or expertise. A sector, domain or realm of a society.

So, when we speak of "**Positioning**", it means that after we come to a revelation of our Call, Purpose and Destiny, the next step is to be Positioned at or in a specific place or sphere from where we will fulfil that Call, Purpose and Destiny.

But before that "**Positioning**" can take place, there must be a locating of that place, an accessing, stepping into and an establishing yourself in that place so as to complete the positioning.

2. YOUR POSITIONING IS TIED TO YOUR PURPOSE

To this extent knowing your Call and Purpose is the first and most fundamental cue and clue to locating your Place of Assignment. So, discovering and knowing why you were created and what you were called to do, is crucial to locating your sphere and place of Purpose and assignment.

The Call you were created to fulfil comes with a place and sphere. Every Woman has a specific ordained place and sphere, area or sector where you are ordained to exert the greatest influence and impact (hopefully positive as opposed to negative). Where you should be positioned and located in order to fulfil your Purpose and Call.

3. LOCATE AND STEP INTO YOUR PLACE AND SPHERE.

This begs the question as to who does the locating and the Positioning?

The divine aspect of our positioning leads you to the next revelation and insight namely that before you can be divinely positioned in your place and sphere, you must obviously be positioned in your Calling and Purpose (in terms of having discovered what you were created to do) so that you then get positioned in your place and sphere. This culminates in your being positioned for Destiny.

Notwithstanding that your place and sphere is already ordained for you, the locating and stepping into that place and sphere is incumbent upon you. It is your responsibility to use the signposts and arrows that will lead you there.

In addition, once you locate that place and step into it then the real positioning starts as we seek to be established in that place logistically and strategically. This will entail understanding the nature, atmosphere and environment of that place, the snags and snares you may expect there, how to properly establish yourself there, how to master the art of negotiation there and the footprints you need to leave in that place as you fulfil our Call.

Logic would dictate that since your Calling leads you to your place and sphere where you will fulfil that Calling, then that place and sphere will have what you require in order to fulfil your Calling (such as the Provision, the relationships, the protection, the grace).

"Be sure you put your foot in the right sphere, then stand firm"
~ Abraham Lincoln

Your ability to locate your ordained sphere of Purpose and assignment is one thing. Your ability to position yourself there securely is another thing. Exerting positive influence and leaving footprints that will impact future generations is yet another thing. We have been called to be the salt of the earth, meaning we should season the place where we are located and positioned positively.

You will need to know the arrows that will be the signposts to finding your place and sphere, then once you locate it you will need to establish yourself there, learn and understand the culture, etiquette and protocols of that place. Master the art of negotiation as you engage with the people there, ascertain. Beware of the snags and snares in that sphere that will seek to entrap you. Ascertain the mountain peaks that you will need to scale, the giants you need to slay. You will need to leave significant footprints once you have fulfilled your assignments there, as a sign that you made a positive impact.

4. EACH ONE HAS A PLACE AND A SPHERE TO INFLUENCE

In any society or nation, there will be certain spheres of influence, sometimes referred to as pillars, mountains or gates for example the spheres of politics and governance, business and economy, media, arts and entertainment, education, family and religion or church etc.

Each one of us was created for a particular sphere and place and it is up to us to locate it.

5. BEWARE OF BEING POSITIOINED IN THE WRONG PLACE AND SPHERE

As a wise Woman of Destiny, you must guard against two common errors, namely operating in the wrong place and sphere or in the wrong position or overstepping the boundaries and mandates of your sphere and position. You must remain planted in your sphere and position, in order to be effective and fulfil your Purpose and Destiny.

6. YOU WILL THRIVE AT YOUR RIGHT PLACE AND SPHERE

Your Purpose is inevitably tied to a place or sphere, a physical location where you will find your identity, uniqueness and belonging. When you get to your sphere, your gifting, talents and skills will be activated for optimum fruitfulness as you fulfil your Calling. At your sphere, there will be a special grace upon you to thrive, excel and blossom and be at your best.

Once you locate and arrive at the Place of Assignment, even those gifts that may have waned and become dormant and latent become revived and resurrected (by just simply you being in your ordained sphere) because at your sphere, you will find grace, favour and enablement, greatness and success.

It is at your sphere of Purpose and Place of Assignment that you will conceive the vision for your Destiny and it is also there that you will birth them.

Your weaknesses will flourish whenever you are in the wrong place and sphere while your strengths will flourish while you are in the right place and sphere. It is at your right place and sphere that you will find your uniqueness and greatness.

"There is a saying that every nice piece of work needs the right person in the right place at the right time" ~ **Benoit Mandelbro**

7. YOU ARE SENT TO IMPACT YOUR PLACE AND SPHERE POSITIVELY

Each one of us was created to positively impact and influence some sphere by fulfilling our Call and Destiny there. Each is endowed and specifically equipped with the appropriate talents, gifts, skills etc. for your specific sphere and place. For example, if your Call is in political leadership, you will possess the appropriate endowment and equipping like great oratory gifts, social and people skills etc. (which of course will require sharpening and harnessing constantly for maximum effectiveness.)

Destiny Questions To Ponder On

1. *What is your other understanding of positioning as regards your Destiny?*

2. *In what other ways is your place and sphere tied to your Purpose?*

3. *What ways did you find most effective in locating your place and sphere?*

4. *Do you believe that one can have more than one place and sphere?*

5. *Have you ever found yourself positioned in the wrong place and sphere? What specifically made you know you were in the wrong place and sphere?*

6. *In which areas of your life do you feel you have thrived most by being in your right place and sphere?*

7. *Do you believe that you have made significant positive impact in your place and sphere?*

Chapter Eight

The Arrows to Your Place of Assignment

Locating Your Right Place

Chapter Preview

1. Your Sphere has a Culture

2. Your Sphere has Giants To Slay

3. Your Sphere has an Old Guard

4. Your Sphere has Ladders to Climb

5. Your Sphere has both Helpers and Haters

6. Your Sphere has Provision and Sustenance

7. Your Sphere has Grace and Protection

OPENING REMARKS

Locating your sphere and Place of Assignment may entail you leaving where you are in order to find where you should be.

To locate your sphere of influence and Place of Assignment there will be certain signposts, and arrows that will enable you to know specifically which area, industry, sector you have been called to impact and influence.

At Your place and Sphere there will be a culture that is peculiar to that sphere. You must sift and sieve in order to ascertain the positive aspects of it that you will align with and the negative aspects of it that you will reject and seek to wisely change. There will be giants that will seek to stand in your way and so you must slay them. There will be an old guard who may feel that you are coming to take their Positions so they may seek to spear you and you must learn how to escape that spear. There will be ladders for you to climb. There will be Destiny helpers to guide you, there will be provision and sustenance to equip you as well as grace and protection to empower and guard you. There will also be Destiny killers that will seek to derail you.

1. YOUR SPHERE HAS A CULTURE

"Our Culture, our tradition, our language, are the foundation upon which we built our identity." ~ **Frank Sonberg**

Culture is the ideas, customs and social behaviour of a particular people or society, a way of life of groups of people the way they do things and integrated pattern of human activity and behaviour, attitudes, habits, values, morals, goals, practices, customs shared by a society – structures, dress style, social standards, traditions giving that society/ sphere group of people it's identity. Characteristics of culture are learned, shared. They are symbolic, integrated and dynamic.

Naturally some cultures have a negative effect and others have a positive effect on the people and society

It is therefore incumbent upon the people and the society to examine that culture critically in order to determine that it does not draw them away from God, good morals and values.

When you locate your place and sphere it is important that you do not follow the abominations of that sphere.

By the time you locate and position yourself in your ordained sphere, you will find that there is already an established culture that is clearly identifiable with the sphere. You must understand it in order to determine what aspects of that culture will be conducive for the fulfilling of your Purpose and Destiny and those aspects that will be counterproductive to your Purpose and Destiny.

"The acquiring of culture is the development of an avid hunger for knowledge and beauty" ~ Jesse Lee Bennet

You must then devise strategies of how to wisely dismantle the negative aspects of that culture and replace them with positive aspects, without creating chaos and without over antagonizing and destabilizing the environment and the people at that sphere.

"Every culture has something to be ashamed of, but every culture also has the right to change, to challenge negative traditions and create to new ones." ~ **Azar Nafisi**

Understanding and adhering to the industry culture of your place and sphere (where such culture is not offensive) will enable you to be positioned logistically and strategically in that place for the sake of your fulfilling your Calling.

Your failure to adhere to those cultures and traditions may be misinterpreted very negatively and thereby prejudice your ability to fulfil your Purpose and Destiny effectively in that sphere.

Wherever the culture and tradition is offensive to you and against your beliefs and values, you must sincerely seek wisdom and the guidance from your mentors and coaches as to how you will avoid being compromised and defiled by the negative aspects of that culture.

The important thing to remember is that at your ordained sphere, there is an answer and a solution to every dilemma you may encounter, if you follow certain principles in seeking a way out and a way round.

"Culture is not an initiative. Culture is the enabler of all initiatives" ~ **Larry Senn**

You must study the culture of your sphere carefully to understand it's roots and genesis and the reasons why it has become entrenched and established. Check whether it serves a positive and useful Purpose or whether it serves a negative and useless Purpose. Does it enable or disenable you from fulfilling your Purpose and Destiny.

Sadly, sometimes you may have developed a hard-line, radical stand with regard to certain traditions and cultures (usually as a result of wrong teachings regarding your faith and beliefs) and you may stubbornly and irrationally become combative and offensive in the manner in which you resist those traditions and cultures (which you may perceive as contradictory to your faith and beliefs) and end up prejudicing yourself and your position there.

So, it is crucial for you to operate in knowledge and wisdom. Ensure you have carried out your research and sought guidance from your mature Destiny helpers before you reject that which you may not understand and thereby jeopardize your ability to fulfil your Purpose and Destiny in that place and sphere.

2. YOUR SPHERE HAS GIANTS TO SLAY

"Face the giants in your life slay them and move on. Do not be daunted by the mistakes and failures in your life." ~ T.D. Jakes

As you enter your ordained sphere you are going there to make a positive impact, influence and transformation. However, there will be giants (in the form of opposition, adversity, persecution, obstruction and hindrances) that want to remain entrenched and rooted. You are equipped, anointed and endowed to slay all those giants.

"God has appointed the giants of your life with the intention of overcoming them for you and teaching you to rely on Him through them." ~ **Adam Houge**

Giants normally symbolize issues or things we consider insurmountable, overwhelming such as fear, intimidation, criticism, insecurities, opinions of others, threats. Basically, anything we feel that may destroy or devastate us or an vicious opponent or challenge. Your giants could also symbolize corruption, immorality, unethical practices and such other vices and evils that you may find at your sphere which you must slay and eradicate.

"Have I not commanded you? Be strong and of good courage; do not be afraid, nor be dismayed, for the LORD your God is with you wherever you go" **(Joshua 1:9)**

One of the main giants you will encounter at your sphere will be a "Goliath" that seeks to taunt you and intimidate you from positioning yourself and taking up your rightful position and mandate at your ordained place and sphere.

This "Goliath" giant knows that once you take up your rightful sphere and embark on fulfilling your Purpose you will disempower and displace every such giant in that sphere as you radically impact and transform that sphere. Your actions in defeating the Goliaths will set many other people in that sphere free to also fulfil their own Purpose and Destiny.

So, when you locate and position yourself in your main agenda is to fulfil your assignments towards your Purpose, but you must be cognizant of the fact that there are Goliaths that will seek to prevent you from doing so and every Goliath that stands in the way of your Purpose and Destiny must be slain.

"David didn't kill Goliath because he set out to slay giants. He set out to give sandwiches to his brothers, and Goliath got in the way." ~ **Rich Mullins**

Unknown to your giants at your sphere of assignment you are not only graced to thrive there but you are also endowed, gifted, equipped and empowered to slay every giant occupying your sphere.

So once you arrive at your sphere of Purpose, you must use your gifting and endowment to defeat every giant there and set the captives free so that together with the people there, you can make a positive impact.

"Do what you can, with what you have, where you are" **~Theodore Rosavelt**

When facing your giants, you must choose your weapons wisely by eliminating what does not work for you (such as your weaknesses and proclivities) and work with what works for you (such as your strengths) and by using what is in your hand and what you have at your disposal. You must remember that once you are at your sphere of Purpose, you have everything you need within you and around you.

Slaying your giants involves confronting them, facing them, fighting them and eliminating them completely. This means that you must acknowledge, address and confront your giants whatever they may be. You must arise and fight and slay all those giants with a view to intentionally finishing and eradicating them completely, so as to enable you focus on your main agenda, which is fulfilling your Purpose and Destiny without disruptions and delays.

3. YOUR SPHERE HAS AN OLD GUARD

"I run on a platform of change. When you make changes with people in entrenched positions, they get upset and angry. The old guard gets in and they don't want to leave." ~ **Unknown.**

An "old guard mentality" (whether in a family, church, institution, business enterprise, organization, society or nation) is the original or long-standing members of a group or sector or industry, regarded as unwilling to accept change or new ideas. Veterans, old hands, diehards, old school, often and commonly referred to as the "old boys" or the "old girls" club. These can be cliques or cartels in various trades and businesses or in various social activities or in various political groupings.

Your Purpose for going to your ordained sphere is to become an authority, an owner and an agent of positive change and transformation. So, you are not going there as a visitor. The old guard there must either receive and embrace you or move out and make way for you.

The "old guard" may fall into various categories namely those who have finished their work there and so must move on and allow succession (but who want to hold on because it has become a comfort zone).

Others are misguided into believing that they are still relevant and valuable there, while others are simply addicted to power and position and have a controlling nature so they want to dominate a place eternally. The worst are those who have resorted to wicked ways, so they want to keep the people and the place in bondage while they continue with their wicked devices impacting the place negatively and protecting themselves from exposure and punishment.

So, they seek to "spear" and kill (like king Saul tried to do to David) so as to silence you before you even start fulfilling your call. Others may befriend you deceptively and then cunningly emasculate you and kill every gift within you, while they pretend to nurture you.

So as a "new guard" you must remember that there can be no alliance with the old guard and you must keep your distance wisely. It is your continued obedience and diligence in fulfilling your Call in that place that will make your stronger and wiser and the old guard will grow weaker and weaker until the old guard is no more.

Typically, the old guard are usually those who have failed to make the impact, exert the influence and effect the necessary transformation and positive change they were to make in that sphere. They have become irrelevant and must move out and make way for you and others like you whose time has come.

"The old guard dies but it never surrenders" ~ **Margaret Mitchell**

This quote means that even though an old guard has ''died' in terms of value, relevance and impact. Nonetheless they will stubbornly hold on to power and positions refusing to give way for a new guard that is more vibrant and innovative more relevant and valuable to take over from them.

You must be wise in taking up your position and escaping the spear of the old guard. Ensure to learn the lessons you need to learn of how not to become an old guard yourself.

Ascertain where they went wrong and the landmines, they must have stepped on that messed them up so that you avoid those landmines. Remember what goes around comes around. Also ensure that you do not erroneously label or judge people you may perceive as old guards without ascertaining for sure, incase their time, relevance and value has not yet expired.

So be careful how you handle the old guard lest you approach them with the arrogance, disrespect and the misguided zeal of youth. There are elders who though stubborn still need to be honoured and because they must have played their role and done some good at one time and the only problem is that they have over stayed their time and outlived their relevance. So be wise because it is wisdom not aggression that will guide you.

4. YOUR SPHERE HAS LADDERS TO CLIMB

Once you locate and establish yourself at your Place of Assignment you will need to ascertain the ladders you need to climb in order to move from one level to another (in terms of getting more and more empowered). You will come to a level whereby you are a Voice at that place and sphere that cannot be ignored and you will become a serious stakeholder whose opinion at that place and sphere cannot be overlooked. You become an expert and create a niche in your area of Purpose and Calling so that your mastery cannot be side-lined. You will make such a positive influence in that place and sphere that you become a legitimate authority who cannot be bypassed and your influence creates such a commanding presence that cannot be erased. Your uniqueness cannot be matched nor can the dynamic positive difference that you have made there be denied. So that your relevance and value will be a force to reckon with and your footprints in that place and sphere will become the building bricks for your legacy.

A ladder has several components namely the rungs i.e. the steps which are vertical, the side rails which are horizontal.

The rungs represent your competence which symbolizes the skills, talents and gifts that you will need, to step up from one level to the next which will consist of your self-growth and development. The rail represents what you hold on to for safety as you climb up the ladder which symbolizes your good qualities i.e. your values, principles, good traits and work ethics that will uphold you as you climb up the ladder to your success and Destiny.

So, in other words your ladder holder who is one of your Destiny helpers holds you accountable to your values, principles, characteristics and ethics as you climb up to fulfil your Purpose and Destiny.

This means that at your Place of Assignment you will need to learn new skills and also harness and sharpen the skills that you already have in order to build adequate competence. You will also need to have a moulded character by establishing values, principles, work ethics etc. in order to successfully climb the various ladders at your place and sphere in fulfilling your Purpose and Destiny.

Having character on its own without competence will not suffice and having competence alone without character will also not suffice and the two must work together for your overall credibility and effectiveness.

5. YOUR SPHERE HAS BOTH HELPERS AND HATERS

"The biggest help God can ever give you is the help of knowing who your Destiny helpers are, and you not losing them no matter what." ~ **Dr. Sonnie Badu**

At your sphere you will find all your Destiny helpers who you must identify and connect with so that they may support you in fulfilling your Purpose and propel you to your Destiny.

"Dream out loud! Your Destiny helper maybe listening" **~Unknown**

Your helpers will include: your connectors, gate keepers, burden bearers, ladder holders, sponsors, mentors and coaches, role models etc. So, when you get to your sphere of Purpose, one of the key resources you'll find there awaiting your arrival are these Destiny relationships that will guide you, instruct you, caution you in fulfilling your Purpose.

"Destiny helpers often appear as disguised as dreadful beggars. May God give you wisdom to discern and honour them." ~ **Paul Bamikole**

Your Destiny helpers will know and help you through the stages of conceiving, carrying, birthing and nurturing your Purpose so that you fulfil it effectively and timely.

These Destiny helpers are relationships that you must guard jealously and keep them close to your heart and treat them like gold as very valuable resources in the fulfilment of your Purpose and Destiny.

Remember that you are also a Destiny helper to other people and your commitment and loyalty to those whom you have been called to help in the fulfilment of their Purpose and Destiny is crucial in ensuring that you qualify for your own Destiny helpers.

To the same extent and measure that you will find Destiny helpers at your sphere of Purpose, you will also find a hoard of Destiny haters bearing the trademarks of envy, jealousy, insecurity, defamation, slander, dishonour, disrespect, sabotage, undermining, mockery, covetousness, criticism etc. who will seek to do everything in their power to hinder and obstruct you and discredit you from fulfilling your Purpose at your sphere.

"When people hate on you, it is because you have something they want." **Unknown**

These haters are not worth your time and attention.

The most important thing to note about your haters is that they have failed to make the necessary impact they should have made and they have failed to fulfil their own Purposes. They are misguided into thinking that by hindering you it might advance them (which is of course not true).

"Haters don't hate you, they hate themselves because you are a reflection of what they wish to be." **Unknown**

Focus on fulfilling your Purpose and assignment without allowing these haters to derail you.

"Expect while reaching for the stars, people to whirl by with their dark clouds and storm upon you." ~Anthony Liccione

You must never allow your haters to distract you so you should avoid wasting your energy engaging with them

6. YOUR SPHERE HAS PROVISION AND SUSTENANCE

"The provision is in the promise." ~ **Derek Prince**

Everything you require in terms of tools, resources, relationships etc. will be at your sphere of Purpose and your responsibility is to locate and appropriate that provision and sustenance and use it wisely as a good steward.

"You make the decision with Vision and God makes the provision." ~**Mark Victor Hansen.**

Once you are at the right place and sphere where you have been called to fulfil your Purpose and Calling, then all the provision and the sustenance you need will be there. Every material resource, every network, association and relationship, every open door and opportunity, every information, knowledge, insight and revelation, every single tool and every single weapon that you will need to fulfil your Calling will be at your place and sphere.

Once you locate your place and sphere you do not need to go out of it to look for whatever you need. The reason we often struggle with lack of provision for our Visions is because we deposition ourselves from our ordained place and sphere.

Whenever we try to fulfil our Calling outside our ordained place and sphere, we will enter into lack and struggle but when we remain in our ordained place and sphere, we will ultimately experience abundance. That abundance may not come automatically and we may need to be tested as to whether we are good stewards and how patient we are in waiting for it.

"That which you give to another becomes your sustenance; if you light a lamp for another, your own way will be lit." **~Nichiren.**

So even when you encounter a temporary lack while in your ordained place and sphere, do not deposition yourself hastily and prematurely, remain there and be patient and faithful because your place and sphere is your place of blessing and abundance.

In the bible when Naomi and her family left their place and sphere namely Bethlehem (because there was a temporary famine and lack) they settled in a place called Moab, meaning they de-positioned themselves. They ended up facing such losses and calamity and it is only when Naomi decided to return and relocate to her place and sphere that she and her protégé Ruth met and experienced abundance.

Your ability to create wealth and provision will happen when you are properly positioned at your ordained place and sphere because your skills, gifts, talents, opportunities etc. will thrive and manifest best in that place.

"Abundance is not something we acquire; it is something we tune into." **Wayne Dyer**

7. YOUR SPHERE HAS GRACE AND PROTECTION

2 Cor 9:8 *"And God is able to make all grace abound towards you, that you, always having all sufficiency in all things, may have an abundance for every good work."*

Grace is composure and grounded-ness, unmerited favour. It is a virtue of excellence and strength and supernatural enablement to operate in your strengths, gifts, talents, skills and to thrive while your weaknesses are starved and overshadowed. It is the ability to do things with ease, elegance and fluency.

The reason that your place and sphere has been ordained for you is because you have been equipped and endowed to solve a problem there and be an answer to a dilemma for the people there.

"Grace means that all your mistakes now serve a Purpose, instead of serving shame." ~ **Mike Rusch.**

At your sphere of Purpose, you will find a supernatural grace flowing through you as you accomplish your Purpose, with a strength and ability that would normally be beyond your natural strength and ability. It is a grace that does not operate in you when you are elsewhere and it only operates when you are at your right place and sphere of Purpose.

Grace is an empowerment that is ignited within when you are doing what you were created to do, and doing it where you were ordained to do it.

When you are in your ordained place and sphere, you are in your element, like a fish in water or a bird in the air, you are enabled and empowered to operate without struggle or stress because there is a canopy of grace over you.

You will also find protection at your sphere of Purpose. So that even though you will face giants and opposition, as you slay and overcome, you will always be protected from destruction. Whereas when you try to fulfil your Purpose in another sphere that is not your ordained sphere you will not have such protection.

"If they stand behind you give them protection, if they stand beside, you give them respect, if they stand against you show them mercy" ~ **Unknown**

There will always be a hedge of protection around you if you remain positioned and grounded at your place and sphere.

"The protection of a man's person is more sacred than the protection of his property" ~ **Thomas Paine**

So, as you lock into your Calling and step into your ordained place and sphere, grace and protection are part of the deal and package.

Destiny Questions to Ponder On

1. *What negative aspect of the culture at your sphere of assignment do you think needs to be eradicated, and which positive aspect do you think needs to be enhanced or re-enforced?*

2. *What particular giant at your sphere has proved most difficult to slay?*

3. *Did you find an old-guard at your sphere, what about you was the greatest threat to them?*

4. *Which part of the ladder was the most difficult to climb?*

5. *How difficult has it been to identify your Destiny helpers, Destiny provokers and Destiny killers at your sphere?*

6. *What opposition might you have encountered in tapping into your provision and resources for your Purpose at your sphere?*

7. *In which area of your life do you feel most graced and protected while in your sphere of Purpose?*

Chapter Nine

The Snags and Snares in Your Place of Assignment

Disarming The Land Mines That Threaten Your Destiny

Chapter Preview

1. *The Cushiness of a Comfort Zone*

2. *The Conspiracy of Compromise*

3. *The Tasty Temptations of the King's Meat*

4. *The Golden gods*

5. *The Fallacy of a False Sense of Security*

6. *The Arrogance of an Arrival Mentality*

7. *The Seduction with Strings Attached*

OPENING REMARKS

Whatever the nature of your Calling and in whatever Place of Assignment you are positioned in, one of the most common challenges you will encounter at every stage and turn will be snags, traps and snares that will seek to ensnare and entrap you so as to delay, derail or kill your Destiny.

Snares and traps are devices or contraptions intended to capture and entangle you through artful manoeuvres. They are tricks to deceive you into acting contrary to your intentions. A snag is a small, subtle, unexpected hidden obstacle, drawback, problem, difficulty or disadvantage that stops or slows you down from achieving or laying hold of that which you are pursuing or accomplishing your intended Purpose.

Some traps, snags and snares are internal in the sense that they are self-inflicted arising out of your own actions while others are an external set-up by others knowingly or unknowingly.

The consequences of these snares, snags and traps is to also make you lose focus, destabilize and disempower you in your journey by making you less effective which prejudices your ability to fulfil your Purpose and Destiny.

It is crucial that you remain alert and sensitive throughout your journey for these snags, traps and snares. Most of which will be very subtle and will present themselves in a very harmless way so that it may be very difficult for you to give them much attention. It is only after you have been ensnared that you will realize how dangerous these snags, traps and snares can be.

Some of the most common ones include the cushiness of the comfort zone, the conniving compromises, tasty temptations of the king's meat, golden gods, the fallacy of a false sense of security, the arrogance of an arrival mentality and the seduction with strings attached.

1. THE CUSHINESS OF A COMFORT ZONE

"A comfort zone is a beautiful sphere but nothing ever grows there" ~ **Unknown**

A comfort zone is basically a mentality or an emotional state whereby you get used to being in a particular sphere and space whether mentally, emotionally or physically, and you operate smoothly with minimum stress.

To some extent, a comfort zone can have its benefits in that it is a sphere where you feel you are at your best. Where you make your greatest contributions and learn what works for you. Answers come easily to you and you discover your uniqueness and difference.

However, because it is a sphere where there are no conflicts, challenges, hardships, confrontations or battles, you may become complacent and stagnant as you avoid anything that may disrupt your quiet peace and existence. In doing so you will hinder any further self-growth and development as you become averse and resist all change and transition that come to stretch and challenge you.

Your comfort zone is an obstruction to your Destiny. Pay attention to what makes you comfortable because that may hold your growth. A comfort zone therefore hinders you from advancing, progressing or becoming successful because deep down within you subconsciously you wish to avoid any new responsibilities.

"Great things never come from the comfort zone." ~ **Unknown**

There are several reasons that may cause you to remain in a comfort zone whether knowingly or unknowingly. One is the fear of the unknown, because you do not want to leave a sphere you are familiar with. You fear change and transition and the responsibilities and possible sacrifices that come with those changes.

Other times you may stay in the comfort zone because you secretly harbour an imposter syndrome where you fear that moving on to a higher level with greater responsibilities will expose your inadequacies.

A comfort zone may also be an attractive place because of just mere laziness and procrastination. You may have a laid-back attitude whereby you do not wish to apply yourself more, or you simply get weary and fatigued by the hardness of the journey and you simply just want to rest. It could be just boredom where you temporarily get tempted to sit back from fulfilling your Purpose usually because you feel sufficiently successful and you therefore fall into the trap of a false contentment. It is at that point you will get entrapped and your attention is diverted to various distractions such as the *"Bethsheba distraction"* which leads you into a dangerous and slippery path.

"We have to be honest about what we want and take risks rather than lie to ourselves and make excuses to stay in our comfort zone." ~ **Roy T. Bennett**

Sometimes it is truths or painful issues that you don't want to face. Coming out of your comfort zone will force you to hear those truths and face those issues. Sometimes it is a relationship that is actually toxic and does not add any value to your life but you are insecure about leaving it. Sometimes it is a cushy job that you do not want to leave because it will push you into new ventures and territories that you are reluctant to take a risk on.

"The hardest thing to do is to leave your comfort zone. But you have to let go of the life you're familiar with and take the risk to live the life you dream of." ~ **T. Arigo**

Worse still it could be your lack of a revelation of who you really are, what your Purpose is and what is expected of you in order to fulfil Purpose and Destiny. This means that you will settle for less than that which you were created for unknowingly and you therefore choose to deposition yourself from your assignment and from your sphere of assignment into a comfort zone.

The sad and unfortunate consequences of remaining in your comfort zone are that you put a ceiling and a limitation to your productivity and creativity. By remaining in your safe space you blind yourself to the dynamic changes and progress going on around you and you may enter into a sphere of self-deception that you are okay where you are. Ultimately you fail to unleash the full potential within you which will adversely affect the fulfilment of your Purpose and Destiny.

A *"Bathsheba distraction"* is bright shiny object that ensnares you once you settle into a comfort zone and complacency and derails you off your Purpose. It spirals you down a path you never imagined you would go so fast that it threatens your very existence and at any rate threatens your ability to fulfil your Purpose.

Do not rest from your Purpose when it is not the season to rest and do not deposition yourself from your sphere and place of assignment even for a minute, but remain focused and steadfast throughout your journey.

The best way of getting out of your comfort zone is to be open to new challenges, embrace necessary change and transitions. Be ready to face conflicts and confrontations by seeking workable solutions. Be prepared to endure and persevere through hardships, sacrifices, persecutions etc. knowing that all these ultimately grow and strengthen you.

Be open to take up new responsibilities and assignments and be eager to climb to the next levels of success and accomplishments. Most importantly know your Purpose for which you were created and understand exactly what it will take for you to fulfil it. Once you have discovered and accepted your life Purpose then all the things stated above that usually lead you into and keep you in a comfort zone will automatically fly out of the window because of your resolve and commitment to your Purpose.

"Life begins at the end of your comfort zone." ~**Neale Donald Walsch**

2. THE CONSPIRACY OF COMPROMISE

"I love how people pretend to have morals but still demonstrate behaviour that shows they don't! The world is full of manipulative people that are only out for their own gain." ~ Unknown

Compromising is selling out or betraying your Purpose, lowering your values, beliefs and standards, giving concessions and moving your own goal posts. Breaching and breaking agreements and covenants with yourself (like your personal mission statements) being disloyal to your goals, dreams and Visions. Allowing yourself to enter into compromising positions and situations or having a divided opinion and stand on issues.

Compromises can either be moral dilemmas, professional, spiritual, financial etc. Suffice to say it involves you changing your position in a manner that questions your integrity, accountability and character. Compromise involves being bribed or corrupted to partake in things that you do not or should not stand for.

You will often find yourself compromising pursuant to a conspiracy with others in exchange for a reward (whether that reward be a favour, a material gift, an advantage, an indulgence of some carnal desire or want). It is usually as a consequence of the fear of men or seeking the approval of men or a spiritual weakness or an immaturity, pride, faithlessness, carnality as well as greed.

"When you have to start compromising yourself or your morals for the people around you, it's probably time to change the people around you." ~ **John Spence**

The unfortunate consequences of compromising is that it erodes your credibility and puts a big question mark in your character and integrity. Often it leads to a falling from grace and you seriously prejudice your ability to fulfil your Purpose and Destiny.

The best way to avoid conspiracies of compromise is to build and establish strong moral, spiritual, professional, business and social principles and values and to have a strong personal mission statement that will operate as your light house. To walk in accountability relationships with people (such as coaches and mentors) who will help you remain in the straight and narrow and against whom you can bounce off issues that are tricky and blurred so that they can help you shed light on them.

Sometimes you may manage to escape a compromise even if it is at the last minute. Yet you will still be falsely accused of having compromised and this may lead to a lot of suffering, damage to your reputation and character. Whether or not you end up suffering and paying a high price for refusing to compromise, the most important thing is that deep down you escaped this trap and snare and the people around you who matter know the truth. Most importantly the God of your Destiny definitely knows the truth and in time as you continue to faithfully fulfil your Purpose and Destiny, your innocence and uprightness will be vindicated because the truth can never be hidden for long.

3. THE TASTY TEMPTATIONS OF THE KING'S MEAT

Usually the "king" who offers you "meat" has seen the seed of greatness and Destiny in you so he seeks to defile you so he can weaken and control that greatness within you and thereby silence or derail your Calling and Destiny.

"Opportunity may knock only once but temptations lean on the doorbell." ~ **Unknown**

The phrase "king's meat" usually refers to anything that contradicts God's will or any unrighteous acts of pleasure, sin and carnal indulgences. This could include delicacies whether food or other luxury items, desirable exorbitant lifestyles and luxury goods, gifts, favours and perks whether in the form of material substance or positions. All are intended to satisfy your greed, hunger, carnal or fleshly desires and indulgences.

The danger of partaking of the "king's meat" whatever it may represent to you is that it defiles you, subjects and enslaves you to the control and manipulations of the king's agenda (which is often contrary to God's will for your Purpose and Destiny), it distorts your true identity as one who has been set apart, sanctified and chosen to fulfil Purpose and Destiny and it blinds you and causes you to lose focus on your assignment and Purpose which seriously prejudices your Destiny.

The "king's meat" also seeks to convert you into adopting strange and alien morals, traditions, cultures, beliefs and values that are contrary to those you know are true and right. It also seeks to emasculate you and disempower you from being effective in your journey to Destiny.

"Our best decisions are often what we choose not to get involved in." ~ **Doug Cooper**

Usually, the causes that may lead you to succumb to the "king's meat" would be a lack of faith in God's ability to provide for you and enable you to fulfil your Purpose. It could be as a result of becoming impatient and feeling that the journey is too long and hard and you feel short-changed when you see others benefiting and succeeding faster than you.

It could also just be a weakness in your flesh and an inability to resist the temporary in order to lay hold of the eternal. Also, where you have lost focus of the Purpose of which you were created or worse still you have not yet discovered or you are not yet clear of your Purpose or even where you

have discovered it and you are clear about it but you have lost your commitment and loyalty to fulfil it.

The "king's meat" is a dangerous trap and snare as a temptation to compromise and feed on that which is enticing but defiling to your Purpose which will lead you to compromise your Destiny.

The way to resist the tasty temptation of the "king's meat" is by purposing in your heart from the beginning of your journey to Destiny (and constantly in the course of that journey) not to defile yourself, and not to surrender to bondage and enslavement that will cost you your freedom and ability to fulfil your Destiny. To ensure that you retain your true identity of who you were created to be by setting yourself apart and remaining separated from anything that smells like the "king's meat".

Refuse to engage in any relationships, conversations, agreements, situations that may ultimately break your resolve and weaken you purely by having entertained any innuendos regarding the "king's meat". Beware of the power of suggestion.

"If you don't want temptations to follow you, don't act as if you are interested." ~ **Richard Evans**

It is a hard temptation to resist considering that your Purpose and Destiny may require you to remain in the king's palace (where you are constantly confronted with this temptation of the "king's meat"). You may be in a family, institution, church, business enterprise or organization where it is the norm for people around you to partake of the "kings meat".

Remember the Purpose why you are in the king's palace is to influence people there towards the right morals, principles and values by your example. So, you must remain focused and steadfast, resisting any greed and carnality.

4. THE GOLDEN GODS

"Idolatry is seeking security and meaning in something or someone other than God" ~ **A. R Bernard**

The "golden gods" in your life refer to subtle idols that you allow and entertain to creep into your lifestyle and upon which you begin to place your confidence and trust (as opposed to placing your confidence and trust in God and other true fundamentals in your life). Idolatry is the extreme admiration, love or reverence for something or someone apart from the true God.

Your idols may include your high positions and status in the society or in the market place. Your power, authority and influence in whatever sector or industry you are in or even in your family, organization and business. It could also be your wealth and material substance, your education and intellectualism or even your outward appearance like beauty, fashion sense etc.

All these things may blind you into losing focus as to where your true worship should be. It is not that these things are bad in themselves, but the place we give them in our lives is what makes them offensive and a snare to our Destiny.

"Idolatry means turning a good thing into an ultimate thing" ~ **Timothy Keller**

Idols are temporary and infallible and once they are no longer available to you then you lose all sense of direction and Purpose. In the journey to fulfilling your Destiny you must be very clear that God is the author of your Destiny.

That he is your creator and that he is the one who decided the Purpose you were to fulfil and to that extent he is your help in every situation. He is your wisdom, your provision and protection, your way maker and he is the only one you should worship, adore and reverence if you sincerely want to fulfil your Purpose and Destiny.

Some of the causes that may lead you to golden gods are whereby you become impatient when the resources for fulfilling your Purpose seem delayed. Where the relationships you should be relying on appear slow in playing their roles and you decide to come up with your own replacements and alternatives (which are counterfeits and not the real thing) and you enter into strange liaisons and covenants which derail you from your sphere of Purpose.

"Whatsoever we have over loved, idolized and leaned upon, God has from time to time broken it and made us see the vanity of it so that we find the readiest cause to be rid of our comforts is to set our hearts inordinately or immoderately upon them" ~ **John Flavel**

Other reasons could include where you feel disappointed in God because you feel you have suffered and sacrificed too much in the journey to Destiny. You feel that God has failed to come through for you in the way you would have imagined and therefore you lose your faith in God and seek options. This is as a result of an inadequate knowledge of who God is and how he works, lack of knowledge of God's word and a lack of revelation as to the processes you will need to undergo in the course of your journey to fulfil Destiny and Purpose.

"If anything becomes more fundamental than God to your happiness, meaning of life, and identity then it is an idol." ~ **Tim Keller**

5. THE FALLACY OF A FALSE SENSE OF SECURITY

"How much liberty do we want to give up for a false sense of security?" ~ **Rand Paul**

A false sense of security is a dangerous trap and snare where you are overconfident (in the negative sense) and you have a confidence in self as opposed to having a self-confidence. There is a subtle difference between the two because self-confidence is a healthy and positive belief in one's abilities and judgments and your self-identity. Whereas a confidence in self refers to a negative, prideful, bloated ego that makes you feel self-sufficient and gives you a big head.

When you have attained a measure of success and you are followed with accolades, recognition and the praises of people and where people may place you on a pedestal you may be tempted to allow it to go into your head. To make you believe that you are more than you really are or that you have accomplished more than you actually have without realizing that people will butter you up and deceive you and tell you what you want to hear for their own selfish agendas or sometimes just to set you up for a fall.

Proverbs 16:18 – *"Pride goes before destruction, and a haughty spirit before a fall."*

Some of the things that may give you a false sense of security and entrap and ensnare you, include your fame and success, accomplishments and milestones, financial breakthroughs and wealth, public recognition and adoration, celebrity status, power and influence and even physical strength and beauty.

You become so sure of yourself that you put your guard down and in the process the enemies of your Destiny, cut off the source of your strength and confidence leaving you weak and helpless.

Sometimes you may be blinded, ensnared and deceived into experiencing a false sense of peace around you. Yet in reality there is conflict and imminent danger surrounding you, ready to destroy you. A false sense of security will lead you to exposing yourself and leaving yourself naked and vulnerable by disclosing and diverging too much information (about yourself, your life, family and business or even about your dreams and Visions) that will become ammunition for your enemies, dream and Destiny killers to use against you to interfere with your ability to fulfil your Purpose and Destiny.

Another way you can be ensnared and trapped is by becoming too comfortable at your ordained place and sphere. Where you deceive yourself that you have slain all the giants, scaled and flagged all your mountain peaks, escaped the spears of the old guard and displaced them and you take off your guard and slide into a sense of false safety and comfort.

"They who can give up essential liberty to obtain a little temporary safety deserve neither liberty nor safety." ~ Benjamin Franklin

It is at this point that the giants and old guard may be secretly conspiring against you without your knowledge. You could find yourself suddenly overpowered by the giants and dislodged by the old guard from your sphere of Purpose. You become disenabled from fulfilling your Purpose and Destiny because you have lost your power, authority and mandate by having entertained a false sense of security.

The fallacy of a false sense of security is in the way you even disregard your Destiny relationships and networks because you no longer feel the need to either be mentored, coached, supported, guided etc. You are misguided into thinking that your resources and power are sufficient and are all you need. Yet you fail to understand and appreciate the power of relationships because any wealth you create and any success and accomplishments you attain will have come as a result of those valuable relationships and networks that God has placed in your life.

"Security doesn't come from money it comes from relationships."
~ Tim Hamilton

6. THE ARROGANCE OF AN ARRIVAL MENTALITY

"Learning and innovation go hand in hand. The arrogance of success is to think that what you did yesterday will be sufficient for tomorrow." ~ William Pollard

An "arrival mentality" is the misguided notion that can ensnare and trap you into believing that you have completed your journey to Destiny, fulfilled all your assignments and that you have qualified to enter Destiny (and take your seat among those who have finished their race). You begin to settle down and show off and adopt an arrogant attitude especially towards those who are still on their journey.

It is a false sense of achievement that makes you stop prematurely before coming into all that you were created to lay hold of and before fulfilling all that you were created to do. You must address and erase any such mind-set and allow your character to grow enough to where you are able to see that you have not yet arrived.

It is a trap mentality whereby you feel you have learnt all that you need to learn, acquired all the wisdom that you need and that now you know it all and you have no thirst or hunger for more. Yet often even with all the knowledge you may have, you may not know how to use it in the rightful way and you need the input and wisdom of mature relationships and those who have gone before you.

Sometimes you may reach a point where you are ensnared into feeling that you have arrived, accomplished or succeeded. You may even imagine that you did it all by yourself and you begin to tap yourself on the back and to give yourself credit and to demand public praise and recognition. You completely disregard those who have helped you along the way and you even disconnect from those relationships without knowing that you have not quite arrived and that there is still some miles in the journey.

Paul the Apostle in the bible says that he continued to press towards the goal for the prize… realizing that he had not reached or attained all. And David also in the bible spoke of how he continued to seek God as his soul thirsted and his flesh longed for God. If such great and accomplished people could feel that way, you must also come to a revelation that you have not yet arrived.

This "arrival mentality" can trap you into losing a lot of ground already gained and to lose you a lot of mileage in rebuilding relationships etc. As someone once said "success often hinders the pursuit for growth and the greatest enemy for tomorrow's success is today's success". So, it is important for you to overcome the stagnation of past and current success.

"Arrogance is an unhealthy ego in need of repair." ~ **Thomas Faranda**

This "arrival mentality" may manifest itself and set traps and snares in your job or business, in your relationships, in your personal development and growth etc. It deceives you to the extent that it blinds you and it becomes difficult for you to admit that you have been affected by this mentality. It happens so subtly and leads you into a place of comfort and mediocrity, further deceiving you that you have it all together, that you've been there, done that and bought the T-shirt.

You begin to feel that there is nothing new for you to learn and no higher level for you to reach. It makes you unteachable and unresponsive to any guidance and direction.

You must remain humble because humility makes you approachable and it allows you to re-evaluate yourself constantly and to remove any chips on your shoulder as you acknowledge and admit your shortcomings and blind-spots.

Whoever exalts herself will often be humbled and whoever humbles herself will often be exalted, so learn to humble yourself and you will be lifted up.

This arrogance of an arrival mentality has ensnared many women and robbed them on their way to Destiny. Hindering them from becoming all that they were created to be and do because it makes you settle before you have really arrived and before your journey is completed.

An "arrival mentality" stifles your creativity and innovation, suppresses your thirst and hunger for anything new and progressive. Worst of all it deafens you to any feedback whether positive or negative, hardens your heart against admitting any mistakes on your part and against any growth and development.

The way to uproot and disentangle yourself from this arrogance of an arrival mentality is to constantly keep reminding yourself in the course of your journey that there is always room for improvement and growth. That there are gaps and deficiencies in your life that need filling. Remain open enough for feedback and be mature enough to internalize and handle that feedback and use it for your benefit.

You should never think you are too knowledgeable or too wise to forsake learning. Your continuous growth builds your security in your identity, which makes you more effective and valuable and it widens your sphere of influence.

7. THE SEDUCTION WITH STRINGS ATTACHED

The term "strings attached" refers to situations where favours or services are offered on the pretext that they are free and out of a sense of goodwill and good faith and that there is nothing expected from you in return. Yet underneath there are subtle hidden agendas and expectations that only come to rear their ugly head afterwards and thereby binding, ensnaring and trapping you.

Alternatively, "strings attached" can be very clear and visible in a situation (where you are mature and experienced enough to read into the situation) for you to clearly discern that whatever is being offered to you comes with expectations required of you and you are quite aware of it (even though perhaps not to the extent and the weight of those expectations). You decide to accept the situation nonetheless, only to find yourself regretting it.

Beware that people do not do you favours and render you services that have agendas and selfish motives attached to it.

"When somebody loves you with no strings attached and no personal agenda, it is the most freeing thing in the world." ~ **John C. Maxwell**

Often it is situations where you are seduced into relationships, deals, transactions and positions (which initially appear harmless and well-meaning and even quite beneficial) only to discover later that this was not the case and that sadly you were just a ploy that was being used to accomplish other people's selfish motives and agendas.

It is important to ensure that in any relationship the reciprocity in giving and taking is pure and open and honest without any hidden agendas.

Some examples of "strings attached" could be where you are given a very lucrative high position or post in a government institution or other organizations and you are given the impression that it has been given to you on merit and on your qualifications. Yet in truth those giving you the position simply want to use you as a rubber stamp to enforce their corrupt deals and transactions for their own selfish benefits.

Sometimes it is in a romantic relationship where you are a single girl and he buys you something as grand as an apartment with the hidden and implied expectation that he has unlimited access to that apartment (meaning that he actually feels he owns it and that he also owns you etc.). Beware and read between the lines and reject any such gift that will bind and enslave you to become someone's property.

Where there are strings attached to anything offered to you or done for you, you can be sure that the price you will have to pay will be greater and beyond what you received. Often it is a dangerous trap and snare that leads to blackmail, manipulation, bondage and control.

"Caregiving has no second agendas or hidden motives. The care is given from love for the joy of giving without expectation, no strings attached." ~ **Gary Zukav**

In summary, remain alert against all the snares and traps that will seek to derail you off the path to fulfilling your Destiny.

Perhaps your strongest guards and defences against these traps, and snares is firstly by acknowledging that they will be there, so you lookout for them. Secondly, develop a strong and sharp discernment, so you recognize them where they do appear. Thirdly remain in strong mature accountability, relationships with your Destiny helpers who will quickly alert you, and help you out of the snare.

Destiny Questions To Ponder On

1. *What aspects about your sphere tend to ensnare you into a comfort zone?*

2. *What instances have you encountered where you thought you might compromise?*

3. *What kind of temptations prove the most difficult to resist at your sphere?*

4. *What golden idols/gods often glitter at your sphere and how have you resisted them?*

5. *What is the fallacy of security you find at your sphere?*

6. *Have you ever been ensnared by an arrival mentality and how did you escape?*

7. *Have you ever been offered favour with strings attached, how did you cut those strings?*

Chapter Ten

Establishing Yourself in Your Place of Assignment

Taking Up Your Rightful Position

Chapter Preview

1. Running the Right Race in the Right Lane

2. Submitting to the Right Authority

3. Adopting the Right Mind-set

4. Embracing the Right Etiquette

5. Nurturing the Right Networks

6. Harnessing the Right Emotions

7. Fighting the Right Battles

OPENING REMARKS

"A good stance and posture reflects a proper state of mind."
Morihei Ueshiba

Once you arrive at your sphere of assignment and Purpose you will need to adopt certain positionings to enable you effectively carry out your Purpose. The responsibility for adopting these positionings is squarely upon you and you must do so by revelation and understanding of why you are there.

Your positioning will need to be logistical and strategic and not only physically but emotionally, mentally, socially, politically, spiritually, financially etc. These right positionings will include running the right race, in the right lane, adopting the right attitude with the right etiquette, nurturing the right networks, adopting the right dress sense, harnessing the right emotions and fighting the right battles.

Suffice you remember that you have every right to be at your ordained place and sphere so you must avoid feeling like an imposter.

A good stance and posture reflects, stable emotions and a general sense of well-being. Posture can be mental emotional or physical, either in verbal communication, facial expressions, gestures, body language and eye contact etc.

Your posture is a crucial positioning which speaks volumes without words and it refers to the way you carry yourself and the message you are communicating as you carry out your Purpose and relate to those around you. It will also entail your standpoint and viewpoint, opinion, angle and perspective etc.

Beware of "postural syndrome" whereby you take the wrong posture for so long, it becomes so hard to adjust it or at the very least very painful to correct and adjust it. Consequently, you must guard against deceptiveness, faking and stubbornness that comes from a sense of self-righteousness.

Brand and market yourself, polish your elevator pitch and always think of yourself as a brand that needs to be marketed effectively. So, define your personal brand clearly, and identify to yourself and to other people what you want best to be known for and focus on your key strengths. Be visible, stand out for the right reasons and be relevant.

Do not be ashamed of your emotions but speak authentically about what you believe and always have a voice and opinion when it matters.

Speak up and stand for what you believe. Seek and speak your truth and always be open to share your opinions and thoughts boldly. Be ready to critic the opinions of others fairly and constructively.

Don't leave before you leave. Be careful before giving up and quitting just because of difficulties and seeming impossibilities. Instead, you should first explore the options available (by thinking and looking outside the box).

As Steve Covey says *"the word responsibility is made up of two words. The first word is "response" and the second is ability"*, meaning your *"ability"* to respond appropriately and wisely in every situation as opposed to reacting erratically and irrationally. Internalize only what is useful and that which you will need to use in your responses because internalizing that which is useless will only cloud the clarity of your response, and the clarity of your intentions.

Do not always believe that others necessarily know more or are better than you. Always be confident in what you know. While you must always respond wisely and politely in any situation, you must not however condone disrespectful treatment or become too patient in over-accommodating the bad behaviour in others. Stand up against what prejudices you, firmly but intelligently

1. RUNNING THE RIGHT RACE IN THE RIGHT LANE

"Run your race. Focus on your goals and God will bring you the right people in your life'. **~ Joel Osteen**

Chances are that you will find certain people at your sphere who think they know what your race is about better than you. They may seek to control and manipulate you into misleading you and assigning you the wrong race. That is why it is crucial that you know your Purpose before you arrive at your sphere where you will fulfil, it to avoid being misled and confused by others.

2 Timothy 4:7 – *"I have fought the good fight, I have finished the race, I have kept the faith."*

There might also be people seeking to run your race instead of their own race out of some misguided notion or lack of understanding of their own race or purely out of an insecurity that makes them think that your race is better than theirs.

"Let's run our race today, if you are feeling weary it's okay. You are stronger than you know right now. And you are going to make it to the finish line." **~ Unknown.**

Your response to such people is to avoid engaging them and instead focus on running your own race. You must however note that discovering your **right race** will require a deliberate and intentional effort on your part using various spotlights, pointers that will lead you to knowing it.

The most tragic thing is to run the wrong race, like embarking on the wrong assignment and Purpose, that is not ordained for you because even if you finish that race, you will have ran in vain. So, you must ensure to run your right race and fulfil your right Purpose.

Once you have identified your right race running it entails pursuing your dreams and goals, by seizing opportunities, and confronting and overcoming any challenges and barriers hindering you.

"Sometimes the smallest step in the right direction ends up being the biggest step of your life. Tip toe if you must, but take the next step". ~ **Naeem Callaway.**

Be ready to silence, overcome and break any social and cultural myths that portray ambition and success as being bad for women. Focus on running your right race and fulfilling your Purpose.

Take whatever risks you need to take and have faith in your abilities and capabilities to not only ran the right race but to also finish it well.

"Race cannot be won by accelerating in top gear, but it can be won by changing the gear at the right time. Timely decisions in life can help win the race of life." ~ **Unknown**

As you ran your right race and fulfil your Purpose, it will entail decisions and choices along the way. The right choices will determine your ability to run and finish well.

At the sphere you have been ordained to influence, there will be several races to be run by different people (who are also positioned at that sphere), meaning there will be several assignments and Purposes to be fulfilled by different people.

It is incumbent upon you to locate your right race that has actually been awaiting your arrival because no one else there has been ordained to run it and no one else there has what it takes to run it.

Your Right race symbolizes your ordained Purpose and assignment at your sphere.

"One should never take the easy road, but rather the right road, no matter how long the travel". ~**Scott Cerreta**

Every race has several lanes, so each runner must discern the right lane. Likewise, every bus has several seats and each passenger must locate the right seat. So beyond locating and positioning yourself in your right race and right bus, you must also locate your right lane within which to run your race (without running in anybody else's lane).

Your right lane symbolizes your actual specific positions and posts from where you will fulfil your assignment.

There might be people at your sphere who seek to use your lane to run their race but because their race does not match your lane, then using the wrong lane will lead them in the wrong direction.

Proverbs 4:27 – *"Do not turn to the right or the left; remove your foot from evil".*

It must be noted that finding your right lane in your right race and the right seat in your right bus is not about choosing which lane looks shorter in the track or which seat looks more comfortable in the bus.

It must be the lane and seat that you know by revelation aligns with your right race or right bus. In other words, the position or post from where you will fulfil your Purpose while at your sphere. So, for example if your right race is leadership then you must ascertain which area of leadership or what spectrum of leadership you are assigned to, is it political leadership, business, social, church or family leadership etc.

As the apostle Paul says in the bible we should not run with uncertainty or fight as if we were beating the air. We should discipline our bodies and bring them into subjection lest when we have preached to others, we ourselves become disqualified. This means that we must embark on fulfilling our Callings confidently and intentionally with a focus as to what we are seeking to attain, which will require disciplining ourselves so that we do not operate as if we were confused without focus.

2. SUBMITTING TO THE RIGHT AUTHORITY

One of the most crucial ways of establishing ourselves in our sphere is by discerning the authorities that we are to submit ourselves under and undergo seasons of training, preparation and equipping.

We will need training, preparation and equipping by those who know better than us so that we can acquire the skills, expertise and competence that we need for Purposes of fulfilling our Calling. And to also learn how to keep our gifts, talents etc. sharpened and harnessed continuously.

The training, preparing and equipping under those authorities will also teach us how to use those gifts and talents and how to apply those skills and expertise.

Those authorities will teach us how to convert knowledge into wisdom. They will train us in the building and moulding of our characters, mind-sets, emotions etc. So that we do not self-sabotage due to an inability to self-control our thoughts, emotions and actions.

We will also learn how to serve others because this will also be a season of servanthood when we learn how to serve the Vision of another. To be loyal, obedient, submissive and patient because we cannot move on to become leaders (where we will be served by others) until we have learnt how to first serve others with the heart of a servant.

In the process of being trained, prepared, equipped and taught how to serve, we will learn how to suspend our own agendas. How to remain in the background. How to receive criticism positively. How to grow from correction and rebuke and how to embrace all the lessons from our training, preparation and equipping so that we can use them in becoming more effective and efficient in fulfilling our Callings and Destiny.

3. ADOPTING THE RIGHT MIND-SET

"With the right attitude, you can inspire and motivate yourself to do great things." ~ **Unknown**

Your mind-set refers to your settled way of thinking your assumptions, views, perspectives, thought patterns etc. which may not always be right, positive or healthy.

So, you must adopt the right mind set that will enable you to operate effectively. This entails basing your thoughts on truth, and positivity as regards your sphere, your position, your race and your lane.

A right mind-set also involves having a right approach and perspective towards hardships and challenges as well as a right attitude in times of success and victory.

"Never whine, never complain, never justify yourself". ~ **Robert Greene**

A right mind-set helps you see the good in people and not the bad in them, it is a mental attitude that helps you see the good and positive accomplishments in your life rather than the negatives and failures.

A positive mind set allows you to recognize opportunities even in the midst of the worst adversities.

"Adopting the right attitude can convert a negative stress into a positive one" ~ **Hans Selye**

It is important to also allow those around you to comment on your mind-set because sometimes you may sincerely believe you are walking in the right one based on your own misconceptions. Hence the need to allow others you trust to vet you.

"A positive attitude also causes a chain of positive thoughts, events and outcomes. It is a catalyst and it sparks extraordinary results." ~ **Wades Boggs**

Receiving feedback from those who matter is crucial for growing your healthy mind set. However, you must guard against becoming enslaved by people's opinions and approval.

Learn to erase wrong mind-sets and beliefs and never try to dress like a man or behave like a man on the misguided notion that you will succeed more that way. Do not try to be a duplicate of anyone else because you are a unique individual and you have what it takes to succeed.

"You will never play the role of a man as well as a Woman who plays her role well" ~ **Unknown**

Focus instead on improving your own unique talents, styles and strengths. Learn to handle negative feedback and criticism without taking any personal offence. How you handle that speaks to your character. Simply learn to apply what bears witness and reject what does not.

Learn to accept compliments and accolades graciously and unapologetically for work well done. Also learn to accept, blame and responsibility for bad work and under performance because contrary to what many women think, inability to accept compliments is actually false humility. Whereas inability to take responsibility and blame is actually a hidden pride.

Never undermine your value or downplay your accomplishments and never minimize the importance of your accomplishments. Instead describe them honestly and objectively and do not deny your own power and greatness, just because those around you cannot handle it.

Do not shy away from shining when it is your season to shine but likewise never try to shine when it is not your lime light and not your season to shine.

Philippians 2:5 *"Let this mind be in you which was also in Christ Jesus."*

4. EMBRACING THE RIGHT ETIQUETTE

"Good manners will open doors that the best education can't". ~ **Clarence Thomas.**

Etiquette speaks to how you behave and carry yourself, how you look and the image and perception you portray. So, it also includes your dress code and your physical appearance. It refers to the accepted or established code or procedure or behaviour in any group or organization and sphere. The formal manners and rules that are followed in social or professional settings.

They are the conventional forms and usages in polite society such as the culture or speech, control over emotions, common courtesy, decorum, propriety and dignity.

Etiquette also extends to how not to disclose and expose your personal life, so keep your personal life private. The enemy doesn't attack what he doesn't know and do not bombard people with information about yourself that they really do not need or even want to know.

Some women share too much on social media for everyone to see. A private life is a happy and dignified life, someone once said.

So, in order to be positioned correctly at your sphere, you must ascertain and understand the manners of that sphere. These include various etiquettes and formalities, so that you serve effectively without breaching accepted protocol and etiquette.

Naturally there may be certain protocols and etiquettes that you are not in agreement with and if your views on these protocols and etiquettes is valid, and you feel that they interfere with your ability to fulfil your Purpose effectively, then of course it is your responsibility to wisely embark on changing and realigning those protocols and etiquettes.

After all, your Purpose is primarily impacting positive influence in your place and sphere, and replacing the bad with the good wisely.

"Today we must all be aware that protocol takes precedence over procedure" ~ **Irwin Corey**

So, there will be etiquettes and protocols for you to observe in order to position and align yourself logistically and strategically (like Queen Esther and the king's scepter). So that you give honour to whom honour is due and you lay hold of every advantage you need for the sake of your Purpose and Destiny.

"Let us work towards not only bringing civility back in style, but ultimately making it a lifestyle." **– Cindy Ann Peterson**

Your ability to understand, embrace and walk in the right etiquettes and protocols at your sphere is in itself a core competence that you must be willing to invest in by attending an etiquette course, broadening your reading etc. It is a competence you will need for fulfilling your Purpose towards Destiny.

Etiquettes (such as your outward appearance, dress sense, demeanour, your speech language, gestures, tone, pitch of your voice, how you address people, use of titles and terms of endearment, your phone use, right conversations like not interrupting, appropriate questions and comments, inappropriate proximity and physical contact, are more important than we may think, in fulfilling Purpose and Destiny.

Properly handled, right etiquettes should not take away your authenticity because proper and right etiquette is sincere genuine and beneficial.

5. NURTURING THE RIGHT NETWORKS

"Behind every successful person there are many successful relationships." ~ **Joe Apfelbaum**

Networking is the art of making contact and exchanging information with other people and groups to develop mutually beneficial relationships.

Heb. 10:24-25 – *"And let us consider one another in order to stir up love and good works, not forsaking the assembling of ourselves together as is the manner of some, but exhorting one another, and so much the more as you see the Day approaching."*

To this extent, to enable you fulfil your Purpose towards Destiny, you will need, various networks (such as business, spiritual, social, professional etc.). More important you must ascertain what are right networks by checking how they relate to your Purpose and Destiny. So, you must ascertain the use, value and relevance of each network and then learn and master how to maintain and nurture them.

Meaningful and fruitful networking will entail ensuring mutual benefit whereby you are not using or abusing your networks, nor are you being used and abused.

"The currency of real networking is not greed but generosity." ~ **Keith Ferazzi**

Right networking assists in attaining your goals as you also assist others to attain their goals. So, help the people in your network and let them help you. Developing the right networks and the right associations at your place and sphere is a valuable tool in fulfilling your Purpose and Destiny.

The right networks will lead you to most of your Destiny helpers like sponsors, mentors, coaches, ladder holders, connectors etc. who will add value as they impact you and help you to grow and develop.

"You can have everything in life you want if you help just enough people to get what they want." ~ **Zig Ziglar**

6. HARNESSING THE RIGHT EMOTIONS

Our feelings, moods, sentiments, intuitions etc. can be extremely intense and difficult to manage. Unruly emotions can cause a lot of damage to our relationships, so we must intentionally harness those emotions, so that we direct them to work in our benefit in fulfilling Purpose.

"Emotion is more powerful than reason. Emotion is the driving force behind thinking and reasoning. Emotional intelligence increases the mind's ability to make positive, brilliant decisions." ~ **Dr. T.P Chia**

This means that properly harnessed your emotions are of great value.

Developing a high emotional intelligence (EQ) is one way of harnessing your emotions. Prayer, engaging in physical exercise in healthy activities and interacting with mature relationships are other ways, including being coached, mentored and counselled.

"The value of emotions comes from sharing them, not just having them." ~ **Simon Sinek**

Unharnessed emotions can wreak havoc and seriously prejudice your ability to fulfil your Purpose and Destiny, especially since you will encounter severe stress, and pressures, challenges etc. that will test you emotionally, but choose to master your emotions and do not allow them to master you.

"I don't want to be at the mercy of my emotions. I want to use them, to enjoy them and to dominate them." ~ **Oscar Wilde**

7. FIGHTING THE RIGHT BATTLES

"We fight too many battles that don't matter. If that battle is not between you and your Destiny, then it is a distraction that you have to learn to let go." ~ **Joel Osteen**

At your ordained sphere of Purpose, you will encounter many battles, oppositions, giants and attacks. Irrespective of whichever Place of Assignment in a society, there will be battles and the only difference will be the nature and type of battles (since each sphere has its own dynamic challenges).

In life you have a choice to choose your own battles, so you need to save your energy until something worth fighting for comes along.

"Being strong doesn't always mean you have to fight the battle. True strength is being adult enough to walk away from the nonsense with your head held high" ~ **Unknown**

In assessing whether a battle is your right battle, you must check whether it affects your Purpose and Destiny, and if so, how fundamentally. Check whether you are equipped for it, whether it is the right timing for you to engage in this battle and weigh its prejudicial effect against the wrong you are trying to correct.

Whether it be a battle within your family, organization, business, profession, church, social group, society or nation, those will always be the questions to consider.

So without in any way suggesting that you should sit back passively beware of the greater danger, the damage, delay and possible devastation a wrong battle can have on your Purpose and Destiny. The danger, damage, delay and devastation that a right battle fought in the wrong timing (without you being properly equipped and without counting the cost) will have on your Purpose and Destiny. Pick your battles because not everything is worth flipping out over.

In short, your right battle is one fought for the right reasons, at the right time, with the right equipping and at a calculated cost.

Know when to walk away and when to stay and make sure that your walking away is always based on principle not on a personality clash because you must walk away from a position of strength and not a position of weakness, says Dr. Herta Von Stiegel.

"Pick your battles, you don't have to show up to every argument you are invited to." ~ **Mandy Hale**

Destiny Questions to Ponder On

1. *Are you confident that you are running the right race in the right lane or sitting in the right seat in the right bus?*

2. *What attitudes have your struggled with the most?*

3. *What etiquettes at your sphere have you struggled with the most?*

4. *What right emotions have helped you most at your sphere?*

5. *How difficult has it been to create and maintain right networks at your sphere, and how useful have those networks been in enabling you to fulfil your Purpose?*

6. *Did you find it difficult to establish yourself in your sphere and if so in which ways?*

7. *Have you ever fought battles that you later realized you should not have?*

Chapter Eleven

The Pebble Stones in Your High Heels that Slow Your Journey to Destiny

Overcoming Your Internal Struggles That Threaten Your Destiny

Chapter Preview

1. *The Pebble Stone Called Self-Sabotage*

2. *The Pebble Stone Called Victim Mentality*

3. *The Pebble Stone Called Bright Shiny Objects Syndrome*

4. *The Pebble Stone Called Procrastination*

5. *The Pebble Stone Called Shortcuts*

6. *The Pebble Stone Called Fear*

7. *The Pebble Stone Called Fatigue*

OPENING REMARKS

In your journey to Destiny and as you fulfil your Calling, you will encounter various obstacles and hindrances, either externally inflicted or internally inflicted which will prejudice you and delay your Destiny.

Perhaps the most challenging obstacles and hindrances that you will need to confront and overcome are the internally inflicted ones. The ones that are within you, whereby you become your own worst enemy and you obstruct yourself (even without any externally inflicted obstacles and hindrances).

Most Women can relate to wearing high heels and walking on a path or road full of loose pebble stones and the horror and nightmare of the damage those sharp loose "demons" cause to your pretty designer high heels. Even worse is the discomfort, pain and frustration that those loose pebble stones cause when they enter inside your shoe causing such a dreadful friction and anguish that inevitably slows or hinders your ability to walk effectively.

The **pebble stone path** symbolizes the rough portions of your journey to Destiny. The **loose pebble stones** symbolizes the internally inflicted obstacles and hindrances that are within you. (The attitudes, mindset and emotions you have chosen to adopt during this rough portion of your journey to Destiny).

As a Woman in the market place in whichever sphere or sector you are in, the daily stresses and pressures of life take their toll on us, (whether it be gender bias at work, financial distresses, the physical, emotional and mental tiredness from playing our myriad roles as mothers, leaders, wives, breadwinners, role models mentors, caregivers to elderly parents etc.) We may come to a point severally when we lose sight of the Calling and Destiny, we are supposed to be fulfilling and we may at that point adopt a wrong attitude and mindset.

It is therefore not difficult to conceive how you may find yourself having slipped into self-inflicted and self-defeating habits, behaviours, emotional disorders and mind-sets. Walking on "**pebble stones**" with your high heels with crooked Destiny steps, slipping and falling occasionally because of those internally inflicted obstacles and hindrances.

The pebble stones of self-sabotage, victim mentality, fear, procrastination, short cuts, bright shinny objects, fatigue and benign resignation can seriously hinder your progress more than you imagined.

"Just like sin will take you further than you ever expected to go, it will take keep you longer than you ever intended to stay and it will cost you more than you ever expected to pay" ~ **Kay Arthur**

These internal enemies have taken you off the proper path to Destiny and the sooner you retrace your steps back to the proper path the better.

Defeating these internal enemies will require using internal measures within you that only you can summon and muster up from **within** you intentionally and deliberately in order to get off the pebble stone path and onto the smooth tarmac to your Destiny.

Your Call and Destiny must become a near obsession and desperation so that anything standing in the way including yourself must be radically dealt with. The enemies within you are often self-inflicted so you must get out of your own way when it comes to fulfilling your call and Destiny.

The greatest motivation to overcoming any obstacles in your path to Destiny is the revelation that you have about who you are and about the Call upon your life. Your passion and zeal to fulfil that call and Destiny will ignite you and provoke you to do everything within your ability to address and overcome every internal enemy within you.

1. THE PEBBLE STONE CALLED SELF-SABOTAGE

Perhaps one of the saddest threats a Woman faces on her journey to Destiny is **self-sabotage**. It is a purely self- inflicted threat that a Woman weaves solely on her own, often unknowingly and unawares but sometimes aware and knowingly, but unable to stop yourself.

"Self-sabotage is an unconscious subversion disruption or obstruction to hinder your own cause and endeavour. You consciously have a desired outcome but you work against yourself unconsciously." ~ **Unknown**

Self-sabotage is best illustrated by the tale of the "**scorpion and the frog**" where a scorpion asks the frog to carry him over a river. The frog is afraid of being stung, but the scorpion argues that if he did so both would sink and the scorpion would drown. The frog then agrees, but midway across the river the scorpion does indeed sting the frog, drowning them both. When asked why, the scorpion replies and says that it could not help itself because stinging is its nature.

Many times, even when we know or should know that a particular pattern of behaviour that has become our nature will prejudice us, we nonetheless cannot help ourselves and we proceed with that very behaviour towards self-sabotage.

Self-sabotage is any behaviour, action, emotion or thought that holds you back from getting what you want by consciously walking in patterns of behaviour and habits that are clearly contrary to what you want to lay hold of or where you want to go.

Perhaps it is a safety mechanism that protects you from disappointments, so you subconsciously hinder what you want from happening, just in case it doesn't. It is ironic and tragic at the same time.

Issues such as lack of self-esteem, self-worth, self-confidence and self-belief, often lead and cause self-sabotage. We somehow do not believe we deserve to get what we are pursuing. It is also reacting to events, circumstances and people in ways that hinders our progress, prevents us from reaching our goals, dreams etc. It includes our inability to manage our emotions maturely and effectively.

You must identify self-sabotaging behaviour patterns by observing and becoming aware of your daily decisions, actions and consequences. Ascertain the triggers that causes you to behave that way (how can you avoid and remove those triggers) to enable you consciously control your thoughts, actions, emotions and feelings.

Ascertain what circumstances your current or past life, causes you to have low self-esteem, worthlessness and lack of confidence. Is it pain, failure or abuse that happened previously which you have not healed from and got over. Is it current pain, failure or abuse?

Check your relationships, are they toxic and undermining you? Are you fulfilled in what you are currently doing? Do not bury your head in the sand and denial, take responsibility and confront every internal giant and mountain that is hindering you from Destiny.

Seek help from experts, mentors and coaches and be prepared to intentionally eliminate self-sabotage from your life for the sake of your Destiny. Otherwise, you will go round in circles around the same mountain and never make progress in the right direction.

2. THE PEBBLE STONE CALLED VICTIM MENTALITY

Are you constantly blaming others or situations for your misery?

…Do you believe that life is against you?

…Do you perceive that everyone is trying to hurt you?

…Do you feel powerless to change your circumstances?

…Do you relish in sharing your tragic sorry stories with everyone who will listen?

…Do you constantly put yourself down and begrudge those who are happy and positive?

Then you need to get off your **"drama triangle"**, and disconnect yourself from your **"rescuers,"** (who enable your victim mentality by purporting to relieve your pain and keep you dependent on them) and disconnect from your **"prosecutor"** who is controlling and critical of you.

Both your **"rescuer"** and **"prosecutor"** keep you powerless, hopeless and stuck.

Instead get into the **"empowerment dynamic triangle"** and hook up with a **"Destiny coach"** who will support, assist and facilitate a desired outcome and a "**Destiny challenger**" who will build you up, encourage your-self growth and self-development into a Destiny victor not victim.

Of all human emotions perhaps the most useless and self-destructive is self-pity. This is Pebble stone in your high heels that is self-inflicted.

Self-pity is as a result of things that may have happened in your past (whereby you seem to find it hard to trust anybody), or you are so worried that people may somehow dislike you if you have the courage to be yourself.

It is an allergic reaction to personal responsibility in a difficult life. A perpetual victim has a belief system and a survival mechanism and so avoids engaging or dealing with life and hurdles and instead over relies on people.

A victim likes being a martyr to avoid responsibility and adopts a victim stance and a posture that she is always right and that people don't understand her. Her pessimism, passive and aggressive stance repels people. "**Burn victims**" are women who cause fires (strife) wherever they go. Strong women do not play victim and they don't make themselves look pitiful, and they don't point fingers (blame shifting). They stand and deal, with issues and accept responsibility.

We need to stop validating our victim syndromes and instead shake off our self-defeating drama, and embrace our innate ability to recover and fulfil our Calling and Destiny.

As a woman serious about Destiny getting over who hurt you or who failed you is crucial.

3. THE PEBBLE STONE CALLED BRIGHT SHINY OBJECTS SYNDROME

These are internally inflicted attention disorders and distractions that often derail us from the path to Destiny and attack our focus thereby sabotaging the fulfilment of our Calling.

This syndrome will target you when you are extremely and highly motivated and you get tempted to veer of your main thing and chase after "**exciting extras**" only to discover they were not worth it. You will have wasted valuable time and even resources and prejudiced your "**main thing**".

This "**shiny objects syndrome**" (SOS) firstly affects your ability to finish any one project, task or assignment properly or at all. Your Calling is comprised of tasks, Visions and assignments etc. so you end up falling short. Secondly, it affects your ability to plan and execute effectively, it confuses and destabilizes your Destiny helpers or supporters whether it be in your church, business, organisation etc.

When you lose focus and become distracted by things that are not related to your Calling it is because they are attractive and enticing or when you focus on the minors instead of the majors. Sometimes you might get caught up involving yourself in another person's Calling (who you have not been ordained to assist) so that you end up using your energy and time away from your own Calling and getting derailed and distracted. Sometimes you may get derailed by trying to change fundamental aspects of your Calling to look like somebody else's thereby forcing your Calling to lose its original shape or DNA and identity.

Once you acknowledge that you have been blinded by this **"Shiny Objects Syndrome"** you must take steps, to remind yourself of your **"main thing"** namely the Visions of your Calling, and get rid of distractions and realign your focus and commitment.

Remain in your own lane running your own race, and make your main thing the main thing.

4. THE PEBBLE STONE CALLED PROCRASTINATION

Procrastination is postponing action or a lack of promptitude. It can be caused also by distractions deviations and diversions and a lack of focus on the main things. This is perhaps one of the hardest internal enemies against your Calling. Sometimes even having discovered your Calling, being equipped and endowed for it, knowing and having the tools you need, you may ironically suffer a paralysis and a complete inability to take the actions you know you need to take in order to fulfil your Calling.

You cannot quite put your finger on exactly why you are procrastinating except you may have all manner of lame excuses. Sometimes it is fear of failing or just laziness. Procrastination will cost you your Calling and Destiny. To overcome procrastination, you must make a radical choice to get out of it and do what you must do promptly.

Sometimes it will entail something radical happening to you like seeing others who were behind you, fulfil their Calling and **overtake** you. This will shake you out of your procrastination. Always remember that there is overtaking on the Destiny highway and it is painful if you are the one being overtaken.

If you want to be set apart and get ahead, talk less and act more. People will respect your results more than your words. Procrastination kills more dreams than anything else and if your Calling and Destiny is important and meaningful to you then there should be no such thing or word as procrastination in your diary.

If you want real change, growth, and progress stop putting off the things that matter to you. When you make excuses, you are denying yourself opportunities to try new things such as business, education, relationships, getting healthy, keeping fit and working out or starting a new job. Some of us are masters at giving excuses, yet we are surprised to find ourselves stuck and stagnant.

5. THE PEBBLE STONE CALLED SHORTCUTS

In this context "**shortcuts**" refer to cutting corners and avoiding the designated and ordained process towards fulfilling your call and Destiny. This is tantamount to cheating and taking unfair advantage while trying to outsmart or act cleverer than the author of your call and Destiny.

Taking shortcuts or cutting corners is to do a hasty slipshod job. It means to skip certain steps in order to do something easily or as cheaply as possible (usually to the detriment of the finished product, assignment or task). So, it is basically an attempt to be lazy and avoid applying yourself and avoid unleashing your full potential towards your call and Destiny.

Fulfilling your Destiny is a marathon not a sprint and it entails a process and a journey. Any shortcuts means prejudicing and compromising the quality and impact that your call and Destiny will have on its intended beneficiaries and the future generations.

Sometimes you want to avoid undergoing the painful process of your moulding and your making (which you know is inevitable). You may try to cut out some steps to fulfil your Destiny, which will be tragic, because a half-baked Calling cannot have the real impact it was intended to have.

Some shortcuts are like running in another person's race, because it appears to be an easier race and a shorter lane. Where you try to use another person's tools to fulfil your Destiny yet those tools are not fit for you and your Calling because you must use what you have been endowed with.

6. THE PEBBLE STONE CALLED FEAR

Fear can be either of failure because you have failed before, or fear of succeeding or fear of the unknown.

- **Fear of failure** is self-doubt that hinders you because it arises from a low self-esteem and lack of confidence, that makes you feel incapable and inadequate and you may also be battling an inner critical voice within you that constantly tells you, that you are not good enough and not clever enough to fulfil your Calling.
- **Fear of success** is where you subconsciously do not want to succeed and be in the limelight for fear of greater responsibilities and for fear of people's higher expectations of you that you are not ready to meet.
Fear can be real and it can also be an illusion. Sadly, enough the fear that keeps people in the prison of their minds is an illusion, because many do not ever understand what they are fearing or why they are fearing.
- **Fear of rejection**, abandonment, criticism etc. is another common fear as well.
- **Fear of change** because you have settled into a comfort zone of familiar things people and places.

"Being aware of your fear is smart. Overcoming it is the mark of a successful person." ~ **Seth Godin**

7. THE PEBBLE STONE CALLED FATIGUE

Fatigue is basically physical, mental and emotional tiredness and weariness that has accumulated to breaking point and unhealthy levels.

This arises following chronic disappointments, failures and discouragements that often lead to a silent indignation, and benign resignations. This results from a choice not to verbalise or talk about your fatigue hence the silence becomes benign. You become silently angry and resentful and you become passively resigned to the circumstances and you quietly give up and quit the journey.

In fulfilling your Calling, you will encounter a lot of frustrations, disappointments, failures and disillusionments that may sometimes leave you depleted and depressed. The mere stress of being you, dealing with daily demands and expectations can weigh on you heavily and totally kill your spirit. Where you fail to count the cost beforehand or to manage your expectations and fail to balance your time. You can reach a point of fatigue until you give up and you start settling for less, because fatigue has the effect of distorting your perception and reality.

In particular where you undergo chronic abuse from people you love and trust (whether it be emotional, physical, mental, social, financial or spiritual abuse). You can develop a broken spirit that kills every dream and passion within you for your Calling and Destiny.

Fatigue can lead to an abortion of Purpose if not addressed. So, you must acknowledge your fatigue and just rest physically, eat properly, take time off. Do a self-stock taking before moving on.

Having sufficient revelation about what fulfilling your Calling and Destiny will entail (such as the cost and sacrifices involved), will help you embrace the process better and learn to endure. Also studying about the Destiny heroes who have gone before us (whether in the bible or history) will give us a good understanding of what others encountered and how they overcame.

Destiny Questions to Ponder On

1. *In which ways have you sabotaged yourself in the course of fulfilling your Calling and how did you recover?*

2. *What preventive habits and behaviours would you recommend against falling into victim syndrome?*

3. *Do you believe it is possible to recover from an abortion of Purpose, if so, how?*

4. *What methods have you used to counter procrastination?*

5. *What do you think are your greatest temptations towards shortcuts?*

6. *What bright shinny objects have you encountered and how did you dim them out?*

7. *How have you dealt with fatigue in the course of fulfilling your Calling?*

This Page Was Intentionally Left Blank

Chapter Twelve

Key Roles of a Destiny Woman

Aligning Your Roles To Your Destiny

Chapter Preview

1. The Destiny-Minded Mother

(Raising sons of strength and daughters of substance)

2. The Destiny-Minded Wife

(Yoking and Walking with a Destiny spouse)

3. The Destiny-Minded Friend

(Forming meaningful friendships that are Destiny enhancing)

4. The Destiny-Minded Working Woman

(Engaging in a productive daily life activity)

5. The Destiny-Minded Wealth Creator

(Creating wealth with a Purpose)

6. The Destiny-Minded Leading Woman

(Leading people with their Destiny in mind)

7. The Destiny-Minded Citizen

(Appreciating the link between your Destiny and the Destiny of your Nation)

OPENING REMARKS

A role is what you do, namely, a function, a position, a status etc. Some roles are achieved through training and attaining of skills, by virtue of having gifts and talents which must be continuously harnessed and sharpened to enable you perform that role effectively. Other roles are ascribed without considering merit but because one has certain traits even though beyond their control so a role is forced on a person in this situation. A role relates to something you do daily, yearly and regularly as an assignment and duty.

Roles can either be semi-permanent or transitory, for example, someone whose role was once a child grows up and takes on the role of a parent or where a doctor is sick and his role changes to that of a patient temporarily.

Some roles are by virtue of certain requirements (like a boy or man cannot become a mother biologically) hence the reason we have gender roles. The concept of gender roles can sometimes be stretched beyond reason thereby oppressing Women in society and relegating them to less empowering and less rewarding roles.

Roles are also frequently interconnected into a *"role set"* complimenting role relationships by virtue of a person's social status.

Roles may be social, biological, economic, spiritual, political, family etc. and they may include being a parent, coach, mentor, employer, employee, boss, friend, colleague, son, daughter, professional like an accountant, doctor, lawyer, teacher, blogger, student etc.

Roles do not define you but they speak to your worth and value.

Roles come with responsibilities and mandates, tasks, duties, etiquettes and a set of connected behaviors and habits, rights, obligations, beliefs, norms, values, principles, challenges, rewards, risks, and liabilities.

Roles guide you in setting your goals and in helping you fulfil your visions and dreams.

Roles can be illegitimate in the sense that it is not lawful or legitimate. Roles can be constructive or multiple roles where one has several different roles.

Role development can be influenced by a number of factors including social genetic predisposition. People take on roles that come naturally to them (e.g., those with athletic ability etc.) It can be by social influence, namely, where the structure of a society can and often forms individuals into certain roles based on social situations which they choose to experience. By cultural influence whereby different cultures place different values on certain roles. By situational influence where a person blames the circumstances around them for their role play.

A role is the behavior expected of an individual who occupies a certain given social position and status. It is a comprehensive pattern of behavior that is socially recognized providing a means of identifying and placing an individual in an organization, society or Nation. A person's role helps them in dealing with the roles of others.

"The roles we play in each other's lives are only as powerful as the trust and connection between us--the protection, safety, and caring we are willing to share." ~ **Oprah Winfrey**

Role expectations include actions as well as quality.

Every Woman must understand the relationship between her various roles, how to prioritize and balance them, to avoid neglecting any one role. She must understand the functions and responsibilities of each role to avoid underperforming or overstepping. To remain within the confines of each particular role which will enable her to understand and meet the expectations of that role. She needs to ensure that each role is clearly defined to provide clarity and alignment and avoid random, ambiguous roles. She must understand the expected results of each of her roles, understand how one role enhances the other. Acknowledge the challenges of each role and understand how to overcome these challenges effectively.

In your journey to Destiny and as you fulfil your Purpose and Calling, you will obviously have some of these roles in your life. Some of the most critical ones will may be your role as a **Mother** (whether married or single), your role as a **Wife** (with or without children), your role as a **Friend**, or your role as a **Working Woman** (a professional or career woman in the workforce), your role as a **Wealth Creator**, your role as a **Leader** in your community and Nation and your role as a **Citizen** in your Nation.

You must have the ability to maintain a healthy balance between all those roles. More importantly an ability to submit and align those roles to your Purpose and Destiny, because none of these roles can be separated from the Call upon your life. Each role must feed, enrich and enhance your Purpose and Destiny.

You must also be able to define the functions that each role comes with namely the responsibilities, the tasks, duties, obligations, liabilities, rights, benefits, expectations and rewards. Your role must align with your Purpose and Destiny and you must therefore ensure that your choices, decisions and actions regarding each of your roles do not incapacitate you from fulfilling your Purpose and Destiny.

"Every role you play comes with its own set of challenges" ~ **Mireille Enos**

You must also then discern the challenges that come with each role (likely to threaten your Calling and Destiny). How you should overcome those challenges so as to ensure that not only do you perform and fulfil your roles successfully, you also fulfil your Calling and Destiny.

The dynamics that come with roles (that every Woman must be cognizant of and learn how to address) include role conflict whereby your different roles contradict, role confusion where there is a lack of role definition and clarity, role strain where your capacity to handle a particular role becomes overwhelming and stressful, role enhancement and enrichment whereby one role adds value to another and vice-versa, role reversal like where a father begins to play the role of a mother and vice-versa or a child begins to play the role of a parent, role failure where one is unable to perform and fulfill a certain role that they are supposed to or that kind of role is outdated and no longer necessary in a particular culture or organization, role change and role transition where for example one decides to abandon a particular career or profession and embark on a different one.

You cannot afford to sacrifice your Calling and Destiny at the altar of any specific role. For example, as one called to lead a Nation or Church, you cannot afford to abdicate that Call on the grounds that you are too consumed being a wife or a mother etc. Conversely you cannot afford to neglect or forsake any role in your life like being a mother or wife because you are too engrossed leading a church or Nation.

Your Calling is intended to incorporate your various roles and create a harmony that will enhance your journey to Destiny.

The various roles in your life therefore are part and parcel of your Call and Destiny, and they are intended to align with your Destiny, where you have taken a role that was clearly not ordained for you, that role will fight and compete with your Call and Destiny with dire consequences.

Unfortunately, a lot of Women often lose themselves in some of their roles or they fail to balance between the roles. They may become so obsessed and consumed in a particular role(s) and in the process they miss the bigger picture and fail to fulfil their main Call and Destiny.

This is often because a Woman may have waited for so long to get a particular role e.g., a wife, a mother or even as a leader, and when she finally comes into it, it totally consumes her and she gives that role more value and priority than her overall Call and Destiny, and she makes it an idol thereby abandoning the bigger plan and picture.

Your Call and Destiny touches a large multitude of people and makes a wide impact and influence. Whereas your roles in life will usually be beneficial to a limited number of people, jurisdiction and sphere. Yet notwithstanding, your roles are as important as your Call and they should be interrelated and mutually enriching and enhancing.

Your "role set" therefore should be a tool for fulfilling your Calling and Destiny

1. THE DESTINY-MINDED MOTHER

(Raising Sons of Strength and Daughters of Substance)

- A Mother's Role and Assignment

"The subject of motherhood is a very tender one, for it invokes some of our greatest joys and heartaches." ~**Julie Beck**

The role of a mother is unique and special and extremely delicate and sensitive as it entails the bringing forth of a life and nurturing that life for Destiny.

The motherhood role therefore is an extremely sensitive and transformative role because it involves taking great responsibility over the life of another, usually a helpless child and so it comes with a great sacrifice and at a high cost.

A destiny-minded mother is a mother who:

...**firstly**, it is a mother who already has a revelation about her own Calling and Destiny and

...**secondly**, it is a mother who understands that the seed of her womb is a seed of Destiny and that her children have been entrusted to her by God so that she may fulfill her God given mandate and assignment regarding them and

...**thirdly,** it is a mother who even though she may not have initially had this revelation that her and her children are designed for Destiny as at the time when she was conceiving and bringing them forth, nonetheless she has now received this revelation and she has begun to align herself to this critical role and

...**fourthly**, it is the mother who still does not have a clear revelation regarding her own Call and Destiny nor that of her children, yet something deep within her convicts her that her and her children were born and created for something more, so she remains restless until she comes to the crucial revelation and she becomes a Destiny minded mother.

...**fifthly,** it is the mother who goes out of her way to seek God as regards the children He has given her so as to understand what Destiny He has for them.

"Motherhood is the greatest thing and the hardest thing." **Ricki Lake**

A motherhood role comes with various tasks, duties and responsibilities. To physically feed her children so as to nourish them with strength and health. To also feed them by instilling godliness, the right values, principles, habits and morals etc.

"Being a mother is learning about strengths you didn't know you had." **Linda Wooten**

It means to teach, train and discipline that child in the way that he should go. To protect that child from his own internally inflicted forces from wrong choices, habits, behaviors and lifestyle and from externally inflicted forces like his Destiny killers, toxic relationships etc.,

"Mother is a verb. It is something you do. Not just who you are." **Dorothy Canfield Fisher**

To affirm, endorse and build confidence in them.

To pray for them and love them unconditionally to allow them to fall and learn through his mistakes.

"There are few more powerful than faithful prayers of a righteous mother." **President Boyd K. Packer**

To eventually release and let go of them without smothering and stifling them as they enter adulthood and become independent and responsible for themselves.

Perhaps the most difficult balancing act of a mother is where she has to continue loving and supporting her child unconditionally (but without condoning their bad or sinful lifestyle) especially when they are no longer minors who are controllable but when they are now adults, who she cannot physically or legally control or restrain.

"There is no way to be a perfect mother and a million ways to be a good one." Jill Churchill.

- ### The Challenges of a Mother's Role

"It is not easy being a mother. If it were, fathers would do it." Unknown

As a *Destiny-Minded mother* and as you equip and mould your sons and daughters for Destiny, you must also ensure to remain on course without neglecting to fulfil your other ordained roles (as well as fulfilling your own Calling and Destiny at the same time).

One of the significant challenges that has made a mother's role more challenging in recent times is the eroding and eradication of some of the positive parenting cultures that were found in early societies.

A single mother will experience unique challenges that a married mother may not (such as the absence of a father as a role model and more so where the child is suffering from a father wound depending on the circumstances leading to the absence of the father). A single mother's relationships with potential spouses can also be challenging to her and the children.

Some of the other challenges that you will face in your role as a mother whether married or single, that threaten your ability to fulfil your Destiny are;

a) Where you have not yet had a revelation about your own Destiny, or if you have, you have not put value on it, which means that you lack the capacity to see the Destiny in your children so as to nurture them towards it.

b) Where you lack sufficient revelation about the crucial connection between your role as a mother and your other roles and you fail to balance them in to the detriment of your overall Calling and Destiny.

c) Where you make some wrong choices and decisions which prejudice your own Destiny and prejudices the Destiny of your children, (for example where you allow factors such as wealth, class, comfort etc. to guide your choices so that you and your children deviate from the path of Destiny.)

d) Where you lose yourself in this one role of motherhood and become totally consumed and obsessed and you treat your children as idols. Where you neglect and forsake anything and everything else beyond your role as a mother, which sadly renders you ineffective in any other role.

e) Where you are alienated or separated from your children whether by divorce or other factors and you lose the opportunity to sufficiently, equip, mould and impact them for their Destiny.

f) Where as a result of the storms of life, you lose balance and you allow those storms to hurl you and disorient you, to the point where you become incapacitated (whether physically, mentally and emotionally) to sufficiently fulfil your own Calling or nurture your children to fulfil theirs.

g) Where you spoil and over indulge your children and you allow them to manipulate and control you or when your own behavior and habits are destructive so that you lose the moral authority to steer your children in the right direction towards their Destiny. An article by Patricia Mawusi. 2013: Parenting and Culture; Evidence from some African Communities, has a lot of valuable insights on this topic and it is well worth reading.

- **How to Overcome the Challenges of a Mother's Role**

"The strength of a mother is like no other. During times of stress, she may struggle to find her way because she is facing her own personal demons, but her child's welfare comes first. She is not perfect and makes a lot of mistakes but never doubt her love. It burns deeply in her heart." ~ *Unknown*

i.   As a *Destiny-Minded Mother* you must overcome the above challenges by seeking God's mind regarding the why God gave you the children, namely the Purpose he intended for those children (and how he would have you raise them etc.) In other words, the one who gave you the gift of motherhood, is the one with the manual regarding their use and Purpose and how you should raise them.

ii. This basically means embarking on a parenting journey, where you are totally dependent on God for wisdom and divine strategy. God himself will give you Destiny helpers who will help you in your parenting journey.

iii. It is because of this crucial mandate that a mother has over her children, that will cause a mother to make the highest sacrifices and endure unimaginable suffering, self-denial and pain etc.

iv. Notwithstanding, as a *Destiny minded mother*, you should ensure that any sacrifice and suffering you accept for the sake of your child is in the right context and for the right reasons (lest in your sacrificing or suffering you become so depleted and damaged, that you are of no value and positive impact to your children). In other words where the suffering and sacrificing is ordained for a greater Purpose, then the grace will be sufficient and you will be preserved to fulfil your own Calling and empower your children to fulfil theirs as well. However, where the sacrificing and suffering is not ordained but carelessly self-inflicted or misguided then it will be in vain and of no benefit to you or your children.

v. In your determination to raise *"Sons of Strength"*, as a *Destiny-minded Mother*, you should accept that you don't know it all and so you seek to learn all that there is to learn about the role of a Mother and more so how to distinguish the thin line between raising a global giant or a village champion.

vi. If your *"Baby Boy"* has any chance against the daughters of this generation, then you need to instil the values that will give him the strength and the wisdom to be the head priest and prophet to his family, the provider, the protector and the one who propels them to their Destiny and thereby he can command respect and honour from his family, society and Nation.

vii. And in your determination to raise *"Daughters of Substance"*, you must guard against the dangers of losing your "Baby Girl" because of your misguided attempts to project and resurrect your own shattered dreams through your daughter. And you must remember that this is your daughter's life and not yours.

viii. You must also remember that this is a new generation and that the rules of the game have changed since your days. You must deal with your daughters "creative freedom" with a straight face in order to maintain your daughter's trust and wisely and tactfully instil in her the values, that will give her the confidence, fortitude, self-respect, dignity and determination, that will greatly empower her as she navigates her journey to Destiny.

"I am a strong Woman because a strong Woman raised me." ~ Unknown

ix. As a *Single Destiny-minded mother,* it is important to plan and strategize how you will deal and handle your relationship with a potential spouse who may ultimately become a stepfather to your children. At this point you are balancing between the welfare of your children and your own welfare (without neglecting either) and the choices and decisions you ultimately make in this kind of situation will have a bearing on your own Destiny and the Destiny of your children.

As a *Destiny-minded mother* (single or married) you are the first role model that your children will have, so that even if they will eventually fall into the hands of other mentors (who will also nurture and equip them towards their Destiny) you are nonetheless their first encounter as someone who nurtures them for Destiny.

A *Destiny-minded Mother* therefore not only fulfils her own call and Destiny, she lays a sufficient enough foundation in her children and gives them a head-start so that whoever else God uses to usher them to their Destiny will have an easier task of doing so than otherwise.

Perhaps one of the most important functions in a mother's role is to pray for her children. We find examples of great mothers in the Bible who prayed their children to Destiny.

- *Hannah (Mother of Samuel) - 1 Samuel 1-2*
- *Eunice and Lois (Timothy's mother and Grandmother) - Book of Timothy*

- *Sarah (Mother of Isaac) - Book of Genesis*
- *Rebekah (Mother of Jacob and Esau) - the Book of Genesis*
- *Jochebed (Mother of Aaron, Moses, and Miriam) - Book of Exodus*
- *Elizabeth (Mother of John the Baptist) – Luke 1*
- *Mary Mother of Jesus - Luke 1:46-55*

Whenever you become overwhelmed in your role as a mother be encouraged by these mothers in the Bible and also encourage yourself by remembering the following advice:

- **Be righteous and faithful**

"There are few things more powerful than faithful prayers of a righteous mother." ~ President Boyd K. Packer

- **Your prayers are powerful**

"No power on earth compares to a mother's tender prayer." ~ Edwin Arnold

- **Your prayers will guide your children**

"I remember my mother's prayer and they have always followed me. They have clung to me all my life." ~ Abraham Lincoln

- **Wage a warfare for your children constantly**

"The battle for our children's lives is waged on our knees. When we don't pray, it's like sitting on the sidelines watching our children in a war zone getting shot at from every angle. When we do pray, we're in the battle alongside them, appropriating God's power on their behalf. If we also declare the Word of God in our prayers, then we wield a powerful weapon against which no enemy can prevail." ~ Stormie Omartian

- **You are a warrior for your children**

"Prayer warrior mother's cover their kids with God's blessings and protection." ~ Marla Alupoaicei

- **Your place of prayer is a safe place**

"Every mother's prayer; guide her to a place where she'll be safe." ~ Carole Bayer Sager

- **Pray for your children without ceasing**

"The bond between mothers and their children is one defined by love. As a mother's prayer for her children are unending, so are the wisdom, grace and strength they provide for their children." ~ George W. Bush

- **Allow your children to watch and hear you pray**

"God does hear and answer prayers. . . From childhood, at my mother's knee where I first learned to pray . . . I know without question that it is possible for men and women to reach out in humility and prayer and tap that Unseen Power." ~ Ezra Taft Benson

- **Pray always instead of worrying**

"During all those years of struggle and heartache, my mother never worried. She took all her troubles to God in prayer." ~ Dale Carnegie

- **Know when to pray and when to act**

"My mother knew when to listen and when to pray and when to help. I wonder how many people knew the compassion [my mother] held for them and how hard, in the privacy of her God Box, she prayed for them and their struggles." ~ Mary Lou Quinlan

- **Your children will never be too grown up for your prayer**

"To this day, even though I am grown and have two children of my own, whenever I travel somewhere distant or am undertaking a major project, my mother will sit me down, lay hands on me, and say a prayer of blessing." ~ Francisco J. García Jr.

- **Plant a prayer life in your children**

"From the time of my earliest memories, she impressed upon me one rule above all others: when I woke from sleep, my first duty was to pray to God for spiritual nourishment and blessings . . . my mother would never relent . . . She planted in me, and tended in my early life, a profound love and fear of God." ~ Sadhu Sundar Singh

2. THE DESTINY-MINDED WIFE

(Yoking and Walking with a Destiny Spouse)

- **A wife's Role and Assignment**

"Of all the home remedies, a good wife is the best." Kin Hubbard

The classic description of a wife is that she is a helper, a supporter, a companion, a lover etc. but beyond that she is a Woman of Destiny.

A *Destiny Minded Wife* is a Woman who chooses her suitor very carefully basing her criteria on a man who will be a Destiny Minded husband, so she is

...firstly, she is a Woman who has a sufficient revelation about her own Destiny,

...secondly, she is a Woman who seeks to understand the Destiny of her suitor even before committing to him in marriage,

...thirdly, she is a Woman who understands that in addition to fulfilling her own Calling and Destiny, she will need to help her spouse to also fulfill his Calling and Destiny,

...fourthly, she is a Woman who understands that her ability to fulfill her own Calling and Destiny will be determined by her spouse's revelation about her Calling and Destiny and his commitment to helping her fulfill it and

...fifthly, she is a Woman who understands that a spouse can either be a Destiny helper or a Destiny killer and more so that he may have initially been a Destiny helper who unfortunately becomes a Destiny killer or vice versa.

"A good wife is heaven's last best gift to man, his gem of many virtues, his casket of jewels, her voice his sweet music, her smile his brightest day, her kiss the guardian of his innocence, her arms the pale of his safety." ~ Jeremy Taylor

As a wife you are intended to be a good thing according to the bible and indeed you are a good thing, a precious gift to your husband and you come with favor into his life. On top of that, you add him honor which he receives from the elders at the city gates by virtue of having a good wife

The basic roles of a wife include taking care of her husband and fulfilling his needs, helping him, partnering with him in fulfilling your joint dreams and visions and supporting him by instilling strength and encouragement, for him to succeed.

It is also to respect and obey him, be available for him as a companion. To keep his honor by guarding his reputation and ensuring that you do not emasculate him or judge his weaknesses because you are a team.

As a *Destiny minded wife*, not only will you be responsible for ensuring that you fulfil your own Calling and Destiny, you will also be responsible to some extent to steer your husband towards fulfilling his call and to enter his Destiny.

"A man's best friend is a good wife."Thomas Edison

- **The Challenges of a Wife's Role**

"He who has found a good wife has found great happiness but a quarrelsome Woman is like a roof that lets in the rain." Andre Maurois

Some of the greatest challenges that a Woman will face in her role as a wife that threaten her ability to fulfil her Calling and Destiny are where:

a) Where she lacks a proper revelation of her own Destiny. Without such revelation she cannot even begin to fulfil it. Even if she has a revelation of her own Destiny, her failure to understand how it aligns with her role as a wife will lead to a lack of balance and conflict.

b) Where she finds herself in an abusive marriage, where the suffering and pain erode her self-identity. Without knowing who you are, it is impossible to fulfil your Calling and Destiny.

c) Where she becomes obsessed and loses herself in her role as a wife and abandons and forsakes the bigger picture regarding her Calling and Destiny and she idolizes and worships her spouse and thereby abandons who and what she was created for.

d) Where her spouse is selfish and refuses to support and propel her towards her Destiny and instead, he selfishly uses her to support him and propel him towards his Destiny because he considers his Destiny is more important than hers.

e) Where she is unequally yoked and mismatched and ends up with a spouse who is not a Destiny minded man. Her ability to fulfil her own Calling and Destiny becomes prejudiced and threatened and she is not able to help him fulfil his own because of his lack of revelation regarding it.

Hence the reason as a Woman of Destiny you must align yourself with a man of Destiny in marriage.

- **How to Overcome These Challenges**

"No man succeeds without a good Woman behind him. Wife or mother, if it is both, he is twice blessed indeed." ~ Maurice Harold Macmillan

i. Seek to discover your own Destiny and dedicate yourself to it.

ii. Discern the seedlings of an abusive spouse so that you disentangle and disconnect yourself early before he kills your Destiny.

iii. Prioritize your Destiny and then balance your various roles as you align them to your Destiny.

iv. Do not idolize your spouse or your marriage status. Remember that your role as a wife is to enhance your Calling and Destiny not to kill it.

v. It takes exceptional strength for a Woman to remain in a bad marriage and it equally takes exceptional strength for another Woman to walk out of such a marriage. A Woman's reasoning for either option is often deeply personal and incomprehensible to an outsider looking in, and the last thing any Woman needs is to be judged or condemned.

What she does need is to interact with other Women that build hope and strength and more so to receive encouragement by those who have undergone and overcome similar challenges, whose testimonies are indicative of the fact that marriage as God ordained it, was intended to be a good thing that would usher her and her spouse to their Destiny.

"A good wife makes a good husband." ~ *Unknown*

3. THE DESTINY-MINDED FRIEND

(Forming in meaningful friendships that are Destiny enhancing)

- **A friend's Role and Assignment**

"A real friend is the one who walks in when the rest of the world walks out." ~ **Walter Winchell**

Friendship in this context refers to plutonic relations between a Woman and female friends or a Woman and male friends.

Friendship is the art of forming attachment, affection, amity, sharing life, being connected soul to soul, sharing interests, similar values etc. between two or more people. It is friendly relations or attachments between people and affection arising from mutual esteem, goodwill, friendliness, and people enjoying a support system, sharing life, laughs and love.

"A friend is a person with whom I may be sincere. Before him I may think aloud. I am arrived at last in the presence of a man so real and equal, that I may drop even those undermost garments of dissimulation, courtesy and second thought, which men never put off, and may deal with him with the simplicity and wholeness with which one chemical atom meets another." ~ **Ralph Woldo Emerson**

Friendships develop through various stages as it moves from casual to acquaintance to deep and intimate and some of the stages include:

- **Role limited interaction** - where it is not yet a friendship, it is where people find themselves together either at a function or event etc. and they just talk about general things politely.
- **Friendly relations** - it is still not yet a friendship but the two people begin to talk on more specific things but both are still guarded and not much personal information is exchanged at this point.
- **Nascent friendship** – this is where a friendship begins to develop, and the communication and behavior between two people begins to change.
- **Stabilized friendship** – this is where friendship has developed so there are expectations and responsibilities between two people and this is where the role of a friendship begins to be defined.

There is also different dimensions and dynamics in friendships;

- There are *friendships of utility* where people relate on a need to basis, and depending on what they need from one another.
- *Friendships of pleasure*, where people enjoy doing things together, going places together etc.
- *Friendships of mutual respect* where there is honor and admiration which are invaluable and there is a deeper connection and deeper interaction.
- *Friendships of challenge* whereby the friends provoke, inspire and push one another to think and behave in a particular way and to self-examine critically with a view to unleashing your full potential. The danger with this kind of friendship

is that it can be intense and lead to burnout, so you must lay terms and boundaries.

"Don't make friends who are comfortable to be with. Make friends who will force you to lever yourself up." ~ **Thomas J. Watson**

The fun friendship - which is supportive, sympathetic and calming. This is where friends help each other not to take themselves too seriously and not to be too rigid in their perceptions. They learn to laugh at themselves and at situations. This is good because then they do not break when the wind of change blows.

The inspirational and spiritual friendship - where friends call each other to go deeper in God and unleash all that is within them to become all that one God created them to be.

"Don't walk in front of me, I may not follow. Don't walk behind me, I may not lead. Walk beside me and be my friend." **Albert Camus**

In understanding the role of a Destiny-minded friend, there are certain qualities and traits that become clearly defined in determining what is a true and good friend and what is a false and bad friend. The good qualities and traits that define a good and true friend are honesty, acceptance and caring, loyalty, respect, trust, consistency, dependable, empathetic and an active listener, supportive, authentic, protective, nurturing, emotionally available and attentive, reciprocal in actions and deeds. A Destiny-minded friendship is also sacrificial in the sense that there may be a price to pay for standing with a friend in a difficult situation.

"A friend knows the song in my heart and sings it to me when my memory fails." **Donna Roberts**

A *Destiny minded friend* is:

...**firstly,** it is a Woman who has a clear revelation of her own Destiny, and one who understands the importance of balancing her friendship role with the other roles in her life (so that why are mutually enhancing and enriching). She also understands that she must not allow herself to be consumed and lost in this one role and thereby forsake and neglect to fulfil her own Destiny.

...**secondly**, it is a Woman who has the capacity to discern her friend's Destiny even though she may not have the full and complete picture

...**thirdly**, it is a Woman who places value and priority on her own Calling and Destiny,

...**fourthly**, it is a Woman who respects and also sees the value in her friend's Calling and Destiny,

...**fifthly**, it is a Woman who understands that each of her friendships should be divine connections, ordained to enable her and her friend to fulfil their respective Destiny. In other words, she must be able to see that her friend has a role to play in her life in terms of helping her fulfil her Destiny and likewise she has a role to play in her friend's life in enabling her to fulfil her Destiny. So, to that extent it is a friendship with a very significant Purpose not just a fleshly and carnal connection,

...**sixthly**, it is a Woman who is alert and very cautious to ensure that the friendship does not derail her from focusing and prioritizing her call and Destiny. More importantly it is a Woman who is able to discern when she has entered into a friendship that is not divine and was not ordained for her and no matter how enjoyable that friendship is (and irrespective of the fact that there may be no visible negative elements in it) nonetheless it is an empty meaningless friendship that does not add value to her Destiny

…**seventhly**, it is a Woman who is sharp enough to realize that even where a particular friendship is a divine connection (and was intended to usher her into Destiny, nonetheless and unfortunately if the friendship becomes toxic for whatever reasons, (instead of enhancing Destiny). Then it begins to prejudice and undermine her Destiny and she must know when to exit such a friendship if every effort she has made to rectify it has failed

The marks of a good friendship also include where the parties are not possessive of one another. Neither is over-needy and they are non-judgmental, each has a healthy self-confidence, self-value and worth so that neither is a victim. A Destiny-minded friendship means it is there in and out of season and the parties are there for one another during the good and the bad times.

The Challenges of a Destiny-Minded Friend's Role

"Whenever you are in conflict with someone, there is one factor that can make the difference between damaging your relationship and deepening it. That factor is attitude." William James

Even the most divine friendships will have serious challenges and wisdom dictates that as a Woman of Destiny you learn how to acknowledge, address and overcome any such challenges. To ensure that you do not damage or lose that friendship in your attempt to refine it and make it healthy. This means that you will need high emotional intelligence, good people and social skills in handling the challenges in the friendships.

a) **Jealousy** (possessive, controlling and manipulative tendencies) this leads to a very toxic friendship which arises where one or both have underlying issues (like insecurities, pain from their past or current, low self-esteem, other dysfunctions and emotional baggage that has not been addressed and dealt with).
"Anybody can sympathize with the sufferings of a friend but it requires a very fine nature to sympathize with a friend's success." Oscar Wilde

b) **Not reciprocal** and not balanced and one friend is a free loader (unfairly using and taking advantage of the other) this can lead to deep seated resentments that eventually ruins the friendship.
"Lots of people want to ride with you in the limo but what you want is someone who will take the bus with you when the limo breaks down." Oprah Winfrey

c) **Breach of confidentiality** - disloyalty betrayals and broken promises especially. Women by nature have a tendency to share very intimate details of their lives with someone they feel they can trust, so when this trust is broken it can be devastating and it can ruin a friendship forever.

d) **A high maintenance** - friendship where one of the friends is over-dependent and over-needy, demanding too much attention unreasonably, thereby suffocating the other.

e) Where one is oversensitive and misinterprets situations and words spoken, so you have to constantly reassure them of your commitment to the friendship which can be very taxing to the point of ruining the friendship.

However, it is also important to check that friends are responsive. They should make time for one another and ensure that there is adequate assurance of each other's commitment to the friendship, so that no one feels left out or unchosen. Otherwise, this may lead to one feeling like they are being "ghosted" where one friend is always rescheduling plans (which could be a sign that one friend is not giving adequate priority to the friendship).

f) **Unequally yoked** – where there are radically different values and beliefs so that you have constant disagreements on very fundamental issues.

g) **Disregard to Destiny** - where the friends have no revelation and no regard or respect for each other's Calling and Destiny.

h) **Judgmental** – where there is criticism and an inability to forgive and forebear with one another which arises from a lack of capacity to accommodate each other's weaknesses.

"A friend is a person who understands your past, believes in your future and accepts you just the way you are." ~ Unknown

"Some of the biggest challenges in relationships come from the fact that most people enter a relationship in order to get something, they are trying to find someone who's going to make them feel good. In reality, the only way a relationship will last is if you see your relationship as a place that you go to give and not a place that you go to take." ~ Tony Robbins

How to overcome the challenges of a Destiny minded friend's role

Firstly, it is important that the friendship role is clearly defined in the minds of both parties and that each has a revelation of its Purpose and significance in terms of enhancing each other's call and Destiny.

Secondly, the duties, responsibilities and expectations of that role must be clearly laid out whether expressively or by implication so that there is no confusion or ambiguity and each can faithfully commit to the friendship with understanding.

Thirdly, there ought to be clear boundaries so that each person can maintain their individuality and self-identity, otherwise it is easy for the weaker friend to become swallowed up and forget who they are and erroneously take on the identity of another leading to an identity crisis.

"The most beautiful discovery true friends make is that they can grow separately without growing apart." ~ Elisabeth Foly

Fourthly, it is important to arrest and nip every problem in the bud before it grows and more importantly to have an openness and free expression so that every issue is addressed and emotions are recognized and dealt with otherwise if they are suppressed the eventual explosion may ruin the friendship forever.

Fifthly, it is important to accept responsibility where one is wrong, be willing to actively heal breaches in the friendships which is a sign that you are committed to the health and welfare of that friendship.

Sixthly, understanding what matters and what is important to a friend is crucial so that you remain sensitive and empathetic and it is also a sign of respect and honor.

Seventhly and perhaps very important is to have a revelation of your own Calling and Destiny and that of your friend and to be deliberate and intentional in enabling one another to fulfil your respective Callings and Destiny.

"No person is your friend who demands your silence, or denies your right to grow." ~ **Alice Walker**

In conclusion, every friendship in your life must align, compliment, enhance and enrich the other roles in your life and create a healthy balance. More so your friendship role must align with your Calling and Destiny.

4. THE DESTINY-MINDED WORKING WOMAN

(Engaging in productive and meaningful activities in the Workforce)

- ### Defining the Role of a Working Woman

"What would happen if we encouraged all women to be a little more ambitious? I think the world would change." ~ Reese Witherspoon

Work is an activity involving mental, emotional, intellectual or physical effort done in order to achieve a result. This includes tasks, duties, projects, assignments etc. in a particular sector or industry. People work to generate income, to learn, grow, develop and be fulfilled to meet new people, socialize etc. to serve and provide value to others.

This role speaks to your work and occupation, whether you are a professional in any of the disciplines (whereby you are expected to adopt the functions and behaviors of that discipline) or a career Woman in one of the spheres or industries or generally a worker in the work force. These roles may change from time to time in your life time depending on your choices and decisions.

- ### A Destiny-minded Working Woman is

…**firstly,** one who understands that beyond her job, occupation, career and profession she has a call and Destiny to fulfil. That her job is not necessarily her call but she must seek to align that job and let it enhance her call and Destiny

...**secondly**, it is the Woman who understands that her job is transient and transitory and that it can change any time (in the sense that she can move from one career or profession to another or from and employment to another) To that extent, her job should not define her

...**thirdly,** it is the Woman who understands that she cannot afford to lose herself and get consumed in her job role at the sacrifice of her overall call and Destiny. That in the even that her job begins to contradict or compete with her overall call and Destiny, then it is that job that must give way.

The functions of a Woman's work role may differ depending on the profession, career and industry and sector. Suffice she will engage herself in the particular role using the competence skills, expertise, gifts and talents etc. required for that role.

She will be required to release her full potential towards making a positive impact on her profession, career, job, employment, sphere, sector, industry etc. and hopefully leave some worthwhile footprints for the next generation.

One of the most fundamental mandates and assignments in your working role therefore is to impact and transform lives positively.

Influencing healthy and productive mindsets, habits and behaviors towards self-actualization growth and development.

To also create conducive environments in your sector, industry, sphere by uprooting and eradicating negative and limiting foundations and influences that hinder liberty, prosperity, health and empowerment of the people in that sphere.

In addition, another key duty and assignment in your specific Work role, is to provide practical solutions to the problems and dilemmas for the people who fall within your sphere. To also provide solutions for the problems and dilemmas associated with your sphere, sector or industry.

Evidence that you are successfully fulfilling your Work role, is to be found in the fruits that you leave in whichever sphere or sector you traverse in the course of your life (and not just fruits, but fruits that will positively benefit others).

Notwithstanding all the above, the key spacing issue here is that not only should you fulfill your role successfully, you should also fulfil your Destiny because your various roles are part and parcel of your Destiny.

- **The Challenges of a Working Woman's Role**

a) Where a Woman fails to balance her family and work life, she will inevitably prejudice one or the other. Since they are both important and critical roles in her life, she will not only prejudice herself but also her family and those who are benefiting from whatever her work entails. She must also learn to balance between this working role and her call and Destiny.

b) Where she encounters a hostile environment of discrimination, gender inequality and even sexual harassment at her workplace. She will become demoralized and discouraged and thereby ineffective and unproductive. This leads to frustrations and sometimes she may even lose or prematurely exit that career, profession or job and suffer in many ways including financially.

c) Where she is encountering oppressive factors such as abuse (whether physically, mentally, emotionally, spiritually or financially) be it in her home or workplace, her ability to be effective and productive is greatly limited.

d) Where she lacks the required skills and competence for a particular work and she has no finances to invest in acquiring those skills and competence then she will remain at the low economic levels in her vocation and be limited in her ability to empower herself or others.

"Be stubborn and thick-skinned because I think even if you are passionate and even if you are really good at what you do, I think you are likely to be subject to preconceived notions of who can do what." ~ Anab Jain

e) Where there are cultural influences and her culture and socialization does not favour the idea of Women working in the formal sector of careers, profession etc. Therefore, she becomes relegated to remaining at home, she is unable to grow and develop whether economically, socially, mentally etc. A Working Woman must be prepared to be a leader at her workplace.

f) Chen Chunhua in her article *"4 Traits That Keep Women From The C-Suite"* dated 1st July 2020, points out that the 4 traits that often hold female leader back are:

-- *Insufficient ambition* especially since women tend to have more non-work-related life goals than men.

-- *Excessive perfectionism,* because in pursuit of excellence, women can sometimes get caught up in their own self-imposed high standards.

-- *Conflict avoidance* – leaders must face a great number of conflicts both internal or external, but all too often women are unwilling to face conflict due to the average female leadership style which is more "interpersonally oriented".

-- *Taking on emotional labour* – leadership requires strength and emotional stability but many women struggle with self-confidence because they often have to deal with stresses not just from work but also from domestic responsibilities making it difficult to maintain the necessary fortitude.

Chen Chunhua advises that to overcome these huddles; do not abandon your dreams, focus on your responsibilities not your gender, recruit people who are better than you and learn to cope with loneliness. This is an article well-worth reading.

- **How to overcome these Challenges**

It is therefore imperative for a Destiny-minded Working Woman to become wise and strategic in how she addresses this role;

i. It is important to master time management skills knowing how to prioritize, how to distinguish between the minors and the majors and how to handle the art of multitasking.
ii. Women must also become vocal and radical in claiming and advocating for their rights in society. For better terms in the workplace in order to be effective and productive and for their input to be appreciated and rewarded adequately.
iii. Women must also arise and be a radical voice in creating awareness and fighting against abuse of all forms whether in the homes or the workplace.
iv. She must also understand the need to constantly sharpen her saw by harnessing her skills, gifts and talents. Engaging in self-growth and self-development exercises and activities thereby investing in herself in order to become more valuable, have a greater influence and generate more income.

"Be brave and fearless to know that even if you do make a wrong decision, you are making it for a good reason." ~ **Adele**

In summary a Destiny-minded Working Woman must allow this role to enhance and enrich her call and Destiny as opposed to allowing it to stifle and smother her call and Destiny.

5. THE DESTINY-MINDED WEALTH CREATOR

(Creating Wealth with a Purpose)

• The Role and Assignment of a Wealth Creator

"Here's to financially independent women, may we know them, may we be them, may we raise them." ~ **Unknown**

Fulfilling your Destiny will require resources and finances and your role as a wealth creator will entail engaging in profit making enterprises and applying your gifts, talents and competencies to create wealth.

A *Destiny-minded wealth creator* is a Woman who:

…firstly, has a revelation about her own Calling and Destiny,

…secondly, it is a Woman who understands that she has been anointed and endowed to create wealth and so she has what it takes to perform this role,

…thirdly, it is a Woman who understands that the Purpose of the wealth she creates is for a Purpose (namely to enable her perform and fulfil her Calling and Destiny, to help others perform and fulfil their Calling and Destiny). That that wealth is not for selfish indulgence nor for self-centered agendas,

…fourthly, it is a Woman who understands that her wealth is not only a privilege but is a responsibility and the more wealth she creates, the more responsibility is upon her and that she is accountable for how she uses that wealth,

...fifthly, it is a Woman who understands that she must seek God as to how she should use the wealth God has enabled her to create as opposed to relying on her own understanding,

...sixthly, it is a Woman who understands that the more she uses her wealth correctly and the more generous she is with it, the more ability she will have to create more.

...seventhly it is a Woman who understands that she must become the master of her wealth instead of allowing her wealth to master her. That her wealth is a weapon and tool to enable her make a positive difference, impact and influence.

"You can only become truly accomplished at something you love. Don't make money your goal. Instead pursue the things you love doing, and then do them so well that the people can't take their eyes off you." *Maya Angelou*

A *Destiny-minded wealth creator* is one who is able to birth great ideas and convert them into money. One who is able to turn passion into profit. Someone with drive and ideas, potential and passion to create something new where there was nothing before. Someone with a knack for making a lot out of very little.

A *Destiny-minded wealth creator* is one who engages in businesses, ventures and enterprises that provide a unique value to the environment.

Consequently, as a Woman of Destiny you will need to be a wealth creator and your greatest motivation should be for the Purpose of fulfilling your Calling and Destiny.

Also, for empowering yourself and others to fulfill and actualize because Money is an effective tool for fulfilling your dreams.

Wealth gives you influence and impact, Wealth enables you to benefit others and as you give you grow, which leads to fulfillment. Wealth is necessary for the transformation of lives, societies and Nations.

Your wealth should have a great impact and a positive influence on people. It should empower them to unleash their full potential and fulfil their Destinies.

Your wealth should eradicate poverty, sickness and disease for the majority. In short you have a responsibility to steer and direct the wealth you create towards the right Purposes and to use and manage it wisely without reckless wastage.

You must have the right attitude towards money and always ensure that people remain more important than money and that you remain the master over money.

Wealth creation entails the use of one's own thought and imagination to work in order to bring something extraordinary that produces great quantities of money. Therefore, wealth creation is working with your mind or thinking faculty to produce something unique that will produce great quantities of money and property for greater good.

As a *Destiny-minded wealth creator* you must ensure that the wealth you are creating has a greater Purpose than fulfilling your own selfish desires and indulgencies.

- **The Challenges of a Wealth Creator's Role**

a) It is often assumed that the role of a wealth creator should be confined to men and not Women. Another wrong assumption is that men are better wealth creators than Women. Yet statistics and observations show that 66% of the world's work is done by Women even if they only receive 10% of the world's income.

b) In other words, if wealth creation is as a result of work, then Women are leading in the world's wealth creation.

c) The value in Women is that they invest in families, communities. So smart Governments should spend more on Women by immersing Women in business/ and commerce and therefore increasing more minds, and ideas.

d) However, the truth is that Women have over the decades encountered various limitations and challenges in taking up this role effectively.

e) Some of the obstacles, hindrances, and limitations that a Woman of Destiny will face are, social conditioning culture wrong perception, Low earning capacity, Fear of failure, fear of success, fear of debt. Discrimination and Loss of earning traction which creates gaps in the work place.

- **How to overcome these challenges of a Wealth Creator's Role**

i. To be an effective wealth creator (beyond your hard technical skills) you will need soft skills that will probably be more expedient than the hard skills. Hard skills are specific abilities or capabilities that an individual can possess and demonstrate in a measured way, otherwise known as technical skills.

ii. Soft skills are personal attributes that enable someone to interact effectively and harmoniously with other people. To handle situations, to remain emotionally intelligent and self-aware. To handle conflict, and solve problems and dilemmas smoothly.

iii. The difference between hard skills and soft skills therefore is that hard skills are technical teachable skills acquired through knowledge and training that enable you accomplish a task. Whereas soft skills are the personality traits within you that enable you to use your hard skills effectively and successfully both hard and soft skills must be constantly harnessed.

iv. Your hard skills operate best when packaged with your soft skills or in other words your soft skills greatly enable you to use your hard skills.

v. The character, habits and business ethics, core values and principles of a wealth creator are crucial to her ability and success. She must avoid any tendencies toward self-sabotage arising from breach of trust, eroding of her credibility and walking without integrity.

A Woman's wealth creator's role is greatly enhanced by embracing certain soft skills, there are many soft skills for wealth creation but just to mention some pertinent ones: -

- **Becoming more valuable**

When what you have to offer others (whether it be your skills, knowledge, wisdom, energy, time, support, guidance, mentorship, coaching etc.) becomes highly sought after. Then you must engage in continuous self-development and self-growth to acquire more of that relevant, knowledge and skills, to enable you become even valuable, more relevant, and wiser and on the cutting edge of the latest ideas and concepts.

Become more innovative, set yourself apart with your uniqueness, think outside the box and create your niche market. This self-growth and development requires you to be intentional and to deliberate and pursue quality and excellence in your area of expertise.

- **Forming Strategic Partnerships And alliances**

You must understand the power of synergy and pool your resources, ideas, talents and gifts together with others. Understand the power of interdependence, networking etc.

Your ability to fulfil your Roles including your role as a wealth creator will require you to form the right collaborative relationships. These include co-investors, business partners and associates etc. Alone you do not possess all the skills and abilities necessary. You will gain more mileage in right partnerships and alliances than on your own

Having people and social skills as well as high emotional intelligence will be an added advantage as you fulfil your wealth creator's role.

- **Mastering The Art Negotiation**

Effective *Destiny-minded wealth creation* will require you to become a master negotiator because it will be about give and take, leveraging, bargaining and bartering. Mastering effective negotiation skills, speaks to your maturity and social intelligence and acumen in a market place. You must seek mutually beneficial outcomes, as opposed to seeking self-centered narrow-minded outcome.

- **Embracing The Seasons Of Wealth Creation**

"There is no short-cut to anywhere worth going" ~ **Unknown**

Destiny-minded wealth creation like any other worthwhile venture is a process and a journey not an overnight - get rich quick scheme.

You need to understand the stages and seasons you must undergo as you develop and grow into a seasoned *Destiny-minded wealth creator.*

In view of the element in riches and wealth that often entices, overpowers and consumes some people, it is crucial that you allow the process. Allow your character to be moulded in the process and your attitude towards money refined (so that you have a strong solid foundation and roots upon which your wealth will be founded).

Destiny-minded wealth creation has seasons, some will be dry, some will be hard, some will be extremely productive and fruitful, some will be for preparation, sowing and some will be for harvesting. These seasons come of course in cycles and your ability to embrace each season, understand its nature and dangers, is all part of the process.

- **Leveraging On Your Area Of Strength**

"A Woman who walks in her Purpose does not have to chase people or opportunities, her light causes people and opportunities to pursue her"
~ Unknown

Fulfilling your role of a Destiny-minded Wealth Creator will require you to understand your own strength, passion, gifts, talents and skills. You should aim to create wealth in an area, sector or industry that brings out your strengths rather than your weaknesses, because it is in that area, sector or industry that you will have a gracing to thrive.

- **Overcoming financial pain**

Your wealth creation, journey and process will have enough of its own challenges and obstacles. You must aim to avoid self-inflicted hurdles like past financial pain whereby you sabotage your current opportunities because you have not sufficiently healed from the pain of your past failures and losses, past lack and poverty.

Sometimes your wealth creating abilities are hindered by the economic hardships you encountered either in your childhood or later on. You feel that certain persons or systems were responsible for those economic hardships and you continue to be wounded, carrying grudges that blind you. You fail to realize that you are now in a position to create wealth and that in itself should heal you from any injustices from the past.

In addition, some women who are in financial hardship, tend to resent other people who appear to be enjoying financial abundance. They miss the opportunity to learn and pick valuable lessons from those who are prospering and to learn how they did it.

- **Operating in justice and fairness**

Another crucial soft skill in wealth creation is having a sense of justice and fairness in your dealings with others when trading and doing business. Acquiring and developing the right and ethical trade and business practices is also a crucial soft skill. This means that your pricing must be fair without using unjust scales and without offering defective or substandard goods. Keeping your word and promises by not overpromising and under-delivering. It is also important to be empathetic, sensitive and understanding so that you are not unduly harsh and cruel in enforcing your rights against others even when you would be justified in doing so.

In conclusion, it is important to ensure your role as a *Destiny-minded wealth creator* aligns and balances with your other roles (and you do not become consumed and lost in this one role to the detriment of your other roles). More importantly that you do not neglect or forsake your overall call and Destiny because you are too consumed in this one particular role.

6. THE DESTINY-MINDED LEADING WOMAN

(Leading people with their Destiny in mind)

The Role and Assignment of a Leader

"Leadership is about making others better as a result of your presence and making sure impact lasts in your absence." ~ Sheryl Sandberg

A person who leads or commands a group, organization etc. So, a leadership role will have titles such as Queen, King, Paramount chief, Principal, Head, Boss, Commander, captain, superior, kingpin, chairperson, overseer, premier, monarch, ruler, sovereign, emperor or elder, matriarch, authority etc.

Leadership is the art of motivating a group of people to act towards achieving a common goal.

A leader is one called to lead, so they possess the combinations of personality and skills to make others want to follow their direction.

The characteristics of a good leader include integrity, ability to delegate, self-awareness, communication, influence, clarity, visionary, resilience, humility, Justice, decisiveness, courage and passion, to mention just a few.

The main function of a leader are to make policy, share vision, set goals, mobilize and guide.

The role of a leader and the role of a servant are interrelated in the sense that you will often be fulfilling those roles simultaneously (so that as you are leading others you are also serving them)

"A leader takes people where they want to go. A great leader takes people where they don't necessarily want to go, but where they ought to be." Rosalynn Carter

A Destiny minded leader is a great leader.

…**firstly**, it is the one who has a revelation about her Calling and Destiny and

…**secondly,** it is one who has a revelation about the Destiny of her Nation and people,

…**thirdly**, it is one who has a revelation that how she fulfils her own Calling and Destiny will impact on the Destiny of her Nation.

In fact, it is very rare to hear of a leader who is not also being led or subject to some authority. This is because even the President or Head of State being the highest ranked Leader in a Nation is herself subject to a higher authority and Leader namely God, to whom she is accountable. So, she is a servant of the people she is leading

Also, the top most spiritual authority and leader in a church is also subject to the leadership and authority of God. So, she is a servant of God and God's people. In other words, you cannot effectively lead without being led and you cannot exercise authority over others without having some authority over you.

Destiny-minded leadership is influencing, inspiring, empowering, guiding, and motivating people towards their goals, dreams, call and Destiny.

It is nurturing people to become what they were born to be and what they were created to do.

"A strong Woman stands up for herself but a stronger Woman stands up for others" **Unknown**

A leadership role comes with serious responsibilities which a potential leader must be cognizant of, before embarking on that role such as;

a) To provide a *clear vision* for those you are leading, inspire, motivate and empower them towards them buying into that vision, embracing it and fulfilling it.

b) To *demonstrate accountability* and good stewardship with regard to resources and thereby set an example to others.

c) To be *trustworthy,* honest, transparent and to walk with integrity.

d) To operate with a *high emotional intelligence,* excellent social and people skills because of the diversity of the people you will be dealing with.

e) To be *protective and others oriented* so that those you are leading may feel safe and secure that you have their welfare and best interests in mind. That you are able to protect them from external and internal dangers, provide shelter and healthcare for them and a conducive environment and atmosphere for them to lay hold of opportunities for their growth and development.

f) To *offer policy guidelines* and management structures and systems for the fulfilment of the vision you have in mind to be able to manage and solve conflicts between the people and offer solutions to problems and dilemmas facing the people.

g) To be *decisive and prompt* in decision making, to weigh your choices carefully so as to make the right ones because your choices will affect many people beyond yourself.

- **The Challenges of a Leadership Role**

"Our deepest fear is not that we are inadequate. Our deepest fear is that we are powerful beyond measure." ~ **Marianne Williamson**

The challenges that come with a leadership role are many and diverse but where you have a distinct call to leadership (as opposed to a carnal fleshly greed for power to lead out of a personal ambition and agenda) then these challenges are within your ability and capacity to address and overcome (especially where you have set and established principles and values that will guide you).

a. Not knowing your Person and not defining your identity.
b. Not discovering your Purpose and Calling and your specific leadership call.
c. Not locating your Place of Purpose – failure to locate your sphere and sector where you ought to perform your leadership role.
d. Not recognizing your unleashed Potential within you – where you fail to know your gifts, strengths etc. so that you may maximize them.
e. Not establishing your principles – failure to adhere to a set of codes, values and ethics that you will use in your leadership role and on which to base your choices, decisions and actions.
f. Not knowing the People whom you have been called to serve and lead – a failure to identify your target group will cause you to purport to lead others who you have not been assigned to lead with disastrous results. People you are not assigned to, do not have the grace to receive and follow you.
g. Not embracing the Process, you will undergo, the cost,

sacrifices and pain that you will need to take in your leadership role.

h. Not knowing the Prize and rewards of faithful leadership will cause you to give up easily when you face hard times because you see no incentive.

- ### • How to Overcome these Challenges

As a Woman in a leadership and servanthood role, you need to develop some sharp senses that will enhance and make your leadership and service impactful and effective.

i. *Firstly,* you must have a deep sense and understanding of the *"who"* you are and your self-identity and being secure in that identity namely your person. This is because leadership requires a self-confident person with an adequate measure of self-esteem value and worth. Also, Leadership is about understanding people and you cannot sufficiently know and understand the people you are leading, unless you first know and understand yourself.

It requires you to know your own person in terms of strengths, gifts, talents as well as weaknesses and flaws so that you may also to recognize those areas in areas.

ii. *Secondly,* it also means having a deep sense of the *"what"* you were created to do meaning your *Purpose,* and in particular ascertaining whether you are leading and serving out of greed and obsession for power or whether you have a distinct Call to Leadership. You must locate the specific target group that you have been anointed to lead because they will have the grace to follow you.

This is because any attempt to take on any leadership role where you do not have a distinct call to leadership and servanthood means that you will not possess what it takes nor the heart to lead and serve effectively.

It is often said that as many people as you have access to influence, is as many people as you have to hurt and destroy.

iii. *Thirdly,* it also means having a deep sense and understanding of the where, you have been called to lead meaning your place, sector and sphere of leadership because you can only effectively fulfil your leadership Call within your designated and ordained place of assignment, so you must be careful to locate that place, sector or industry where your leadership role is ordained and intended.

iv. *Fourthly,* you must have a deep sense and understanding of that which is available within you, to enable you lead, meaning the unleashed potential and power. This is because failure to unleash your full potential will make your leadership role ineffective and mediocre. Your failure to harness the power available to you will make you abuse and corrupt that power and fail miserably in your leadership role.

v. *Fifthly,* a deep sense and understanding of the "which", meaning, the principles *(personal core-values, ethics and principles* that you will guide you, in your leadership role and which will inform your choices, decisions and actions. This is because your leadership role must be founded on an impeccable character and integrity. Failing which you will mislead and derail those you are supposed to be leading and directing to their Destiny.

vi. *Sixthly,* a deep sense and understanding of "the whom", meaning the people that you have been called to lead and serve, (namely your followers, assignees, congregants, members, citizens etc.) You are not called as a leader to everyone and you must identify your designated target people. A deep sense and understanding of your Destiny helpers and connect to them. In addition, you must also identify your Destiny killers and silence them.

vii. Seventhly, a deep sense and understanding of the ''which'' meaning the process you will undergo and the price that you will need to pay in your leadership and servanthood role. This is because a Leader must undergo a painful process of moulding and making to become a seasoned Leader.

viii. Eighthly, a deep sense and understanding of the "what" meaning the "prize" that you will lay hold of once you have faithfully fulfilled your leadership cal. This includes the legacy you will leave after transforming and impacting generations so positively.

An excellent example is Queen Esther in the bible. She is a Woman who developed the above 8 senses of leadership because;

- ...she sensed and understood who she was, namely her person and that she was the queen who the king had chosen and she was secure in that identity.
- ...she sensed and understood why she had to arise, because she realized that she had a Purpose to fulfil.
- ...She sensed and understood where she was to arise, namely the place because she was in the palace for such a time as this.
- ...She sensed and understood for whom she had to arise, namely her people with whom she identified.
- ...She sensed and understood what was within her namely, her great potential, authority and power because of the position she held as queen.
- ...She sensed and understood how she would operate based on her principles (core values and ethics) because she understood what she was standing for and what she believed in.
- ...She sensed and understood which risks were involved and the price which she would have to pay namely the

process she would need to undergo and she embraced it.

- …She sensed and understood what lay ahead of her once she had fulfilled her task faithfully, namely the prize and the rewards that came with the victory.

In her article "*Female Leadership in a Male-Dominated World*", Dr Herta Von Stiegel, author, board member, former investment banker and executive chair of Ariya Capital; C200 member since 2004, explores the challenges women face and gives some invaluable wisdom on how to overcome these challenges such as:

-- *Recognizing* that male and female brains are wired differently and that we respond to crisis differently, and that we do not need "fixing" to fit in, is a major step forward to becoming and being authentic leaders.

-- *Recognizing* that how we treat men, how we speak to them and how we hold them accountable will determine to a large extent whether they will accept and respect us as equals (or in some cases as their superiors).

-- *Agreeing* to bring the men with us, because alignment with men can happen not by criticism or complaining, but rather as a result of wise counsel and clearly identified common Cause.

-- *Treating* other women as our best allies, not as our competition, meaning we need to embrace the notion that there is enough room at the top for all of us and be very intentional about helping other women in the climb to their individual summits.

This is an article well worth reading.

In summary, evidence that you have successfully fulfilled your Leadership and role, will be found in the fact that the people you were leading have fulfilled their Destiny, and that the organization sphere, society or Nation that you were leading has also fulfilled its ordained mandate and Destiny.

7. THE DESTINY-MINDED CITIZEN

(Appreciating the link between your Destiny and the Destiny of Your Nation)

The Role and Assignment of a Citizen

"Healthy citizens are the greatest assets any country can have." **~ Winston Churchill**

As a citizen you are a legally organized subject or inhabitant of a Nation whether as a native, naturalized or through acquired status.

So, your Citizenship means that you are a person recognized under the customs and laws as being a legal member or belonging to a particular Nation.

You are entitled to enjoy all the rights and privileges granted by that Nation but at the same time (and this is where many miss the point) you are obligated to obey its laws and to fulfill your duties as called upon.

As a good citizen you should possess a patriotic spirit or patriotism meaning that you are bound to feelings of National loyalty because of an intense and passionate love for your Nation.

"Your pride for your country should not come after your country becomes great, your country becomes great because of your pride in it." **~ Idowu Koyenikan**

It therefore goes without saying that as a patriotic citizen your fundamental mandate and assignments include speaking positively about your Nation. Boldly protecting and defending it. Obeying the God ordained leaders in your Nation. Advocating for positive change where necessary using constructive means as opposed to destructive means.

Patriotism entails promoting the welfare of your Nation by fulfilling your duties and responsibilities including your moral civic and social duties and looking out for the welfare of your fellow citizens. Above all a good patriotic citizen prays for her Nation.

"Never doubt that a small group of thoughtful, committed citizens can change the world, indeed, it is the only thing that ever has." **Margaret Mead**

Evidence that you have fulfilled your role as a patriotic citizen will be found in your sacrificial service to your society and Nation by putting your own personal interests and agendas secondary to those of your Nation.

"I am true to my own race. I wish to see all done that can be done, for their encouragement, to assist them in acquiring property, in becoming intelligent, enlightened, useful, valuable citizens." **Hiram Rhodes Revels**

Firstly, as a Destiny-Minded patriotic citizen, you should already have a revelation that your Nation has a Destiny of its own to fulfil.

Secondly, that your Nation's ability to fulfil that Destiny is dependent on you and every other citizen playing their role faithfully and intentionally

Thirdly, an even deeper revelation that you should have, is that your Nation's failure to fulfil its Destiny, actually affects your ability to fulfil your own Destiny.

Fourthly, that your Destiny and the Destiny of your Nation are inevitably intertwined and inseparable so a "failed state" is a "failed you".

Fifthly, your Purpose and Destiny are part and parcel of a bigger plan, namely that of your Nation and its Destiny.

The misguided notion that you can fight and undermine your Nation's welfare to promote your own selfish ambitions and agendas (by either engaging in corrupt practices, mismanagement of resources, abuse of office and destruction of vital institutions) is perhaps one of the most heinous and unforgivable injustices you can commit as a citizen of any Nation.

"The city is what it is because our citizens are what they are." Plato

The Challenges of a Citizen's Role

"Show me the heroes that the youth of your country look up to, and I will tell you the future of your country." **Idowu Koyenikan**

a. Where there is bad leadership and poor governance of whatever nature, it becomes difficult for a citizen to effectively perform their own role even when they sincerely and genuinely desire to do so.

b. Where there is dictatorship and oppression by the leadership in whatever sphere and where there is discrimination of the marginalized (the poor, the weak, the widows and orphans, the illiterate and the young and helpless) then a citizen's ability to perform their role is also curtailed.
   "There are no necessary evils in government. Its evils exist only in its abuses." Andrew Jackson

c. Where there is corruption, abuse of office, bad stewardship, mismanagement of resources, economic hardships, greed for resources, economic oppression. Greed for power and positions by the leadership (who neglect their duty and responsibility towards the citizenry) then an otherwise well-meaning citizen may become discouraged and disillusioned.

"Corruption is worse than prostitution. The latter might endanger the morals of an individual, the former invariably endangers the morals of the entire country." Karl Kraus

d. Where there are *unmet expectations*, broken promises and unfulfilled pledges by the leadership and by the system. Where National goals and policies are not fulfilled or aligned to the welfare of the citizens, then any citizen will find it difficult to remain loyal and faithful.

e. Where there is *racisms, tribalism, ethnic divisions,* political isolation, bias and inequalities then a citizen will feel helpless especially where these vices touch on them personally.

f. Where there is chronic social ills in the society, breakdown of social and family values. Where institutions like churches become defiled and contaminated, a citizen may lose hope and trust and thereby become unmotivated to do their part.

g. Where there is *delay and denial of Justice* which the laws are selective and ambiguous thereby creating confusion and gross injustices, citizens feel unprotected by their own leaders and governments thereby making it difficult for them to be patriotic

How to Overcome the Challenges of a Destiny Minded Citizen

"A nation's worth lies not in the value of its currency, but in the character of its people." Abhijit Naskar

As a Destiny minded citizen and knowing that your own Calling and Destiny is connected to the Destiny of your Nation, then you cannot afford to ignore this vices that challenge your ability to be a good patriotic citizen.

You cannot afford to take a back seat and give up and more importantly you cannot afford to agree with and align yourself and become part of a defective toxic leadership and system.

It is imperative upon you as a Destiny minded citizen to have a deep concern for the welfare of your Nation and to ask yourself what you can do and how your role as a citizen can help eradicate these vices in your Nation. However, you must keep in mind that different citizens have been anointed and endowed with different gifts, talents and skills to bring solutions to specific areas in a Nation.

So, the first thing you must seek to ascertain is what area in your Nation are you anointed and endowed to release healing and bring solutions to. Is it the sphere of politics and governance, the business and economy, education, media, arts and entertainment, church and family. This is because any attempt to involve yourself in an area which you are not graced for will be in vain.

One of the most important things to ensure so as to make you effective in addressing and overcoming these challenges is that your heart is for your Nation and your desire is for the healing of the Nation (as opposed to becoming vindictive and negative and working towards the destruction of your Nation).

- **Identification repentance** – identifying yourself with the wrongs in the society and Nation and acknowledging that you might also be part of the problem will enable you to intervene and even intercede in prayer for your Nation (like Daniel did in Daniel 9). Also identifying the specific wrongs and vices in your society and Nation is the first step. Understanding why it is a wrong and a vice is also equally important lest you personalize what you feel in your opinion is a wrong and a vice (and thereby embark on a solo, vain mission that is unsupported by any other citizen).

- **Creating Awareness** – calling out and creating awareness about the vices, woes and wrongs using appropriate forums and platforms as well as the right modes and methods.
- **Constructive Feedback** – offering constructive criticism as well as solutions to the challenges is a sign of your positive proactivity whereby you are not just criticizing and condemning.
- **Positive Advocacy** – join others in advocating for better governance, share opinions, views and solutions with others so that it is a collective exercise rather than it being an individual crusade. Be ready to pay a price, incur losses in fighting for and advocating for social and economic justice because it will definitely involve certain sacrifices so you must count the cost in advance lest you embark and then give up halfway and lose your credibility.
- **The Power of your vote** – perhaps most importantly is to ensure that you vote in the various elections whether it be for grassroots leadership or National and in whichever sphere of influence it may be in. Beyond voting ensure you do your due diligence and vote in the right leadership. This is because you cannot purport to criticize a leadership in whichever sphere or level where you have forsaken your constitutional right to exercise your vote.

"A nation of sheep will soon have a government of wolves." ~ **Edward R. Murrow**

Destiny Questions To Ponder On

1. *Which aspect of your role as a mother have you found most difficult?*

2. *Which aspect of your role as a wife have you found most difficult?*

3. *Which aspect of your role as a friend have you found most difficult?*

4. *Which aspect of your role as a working woman have you found most difficult?*

5. *Which aspect of your role as a wealth creator have you found most difficult?*

6. *Which aspect of your role as a leader have you found most difficult?*

7. *Which aspect of your role as a citizen have you found most difficult?*

Words Have Power

Inspirational Quotes And Scriptures About The Woman Of Destiny

<u>Inspirational Quotes and Scriptures About the Woman of Destiny</u>

"Strong women not only feel pain, they accept it, they learn from it and fight through it. They turn their wounds into wisdom. They may fall, but they always get back up, dust off, and fight like they have never fought before." By **Unknown**

"A woman who is at rest with herself has nothing to prove to others, she embraces her strengths & cheers others on with a pure heart. Her light shines brightly; her words are seasoned with kindness, goodness & grace. She is peaceful & edifies others as she is secure in her Heavenly Father." By **Hanna Bryant**

"God has a purpose for your pain, a reason for your struggle and a reward for your faithfulness. Trust Him and don't give." By **Dave Willis**

"She may be quiet, but she's a warrior and her prayers can move mountains." **Unknown**

"She is not broken anymore, she is stronger, wiser and more beautiful than before, because God took her broken pieces and made her new again." By **Unknown**

"Though my soul may set in darkness, it will rise in perfect light; I have loved the stars too fondly to be fearful of the night." By **Sarah Williams**

"In the end, she became more than she was expected. She became the journey, and like all journeys, she did not end, she just simply changed directions and kept going." By **R.M. Drake**

"Mirror! Mirror! on the wall, I'll always get up after I fall. And whether I run, walk or have to crawl, I'll set my goals and achieve them all." By **Brie Edison**

"*I am a strong woman because a strong woman raised me.*" By **Unknown**

"*We all have an unsuspected reserve of strength inside that emerges when life puts us to test.*" By **Isabel Allende**

"*Keep your head up. God gives his hardest battles to his strongest soldiers.*" By **Unknown**

"*If you feel like you are losing everything, remember that trees lose their leaves every year and they still stand tall and wait for better days to come.*" By **Unknown**

"*Strength grows in the moments when you think you can't go on, but you keep going anyway.*" By **Unknown**

"*Some women are lost in the fire. Some women are built from it.*" By **Michelle K**

"*I know you're tired, you're fed up, you're so close to breaking, but there is strength within you even when you feel weak. Keep fighting.* By **Unknown**

"*Strength doesn't come from what you can do. It comes from overcoming the things you once thought you couldn't.* By **Rikki Rogers**

"*It's actually pretty simple. Either you do it, or you don't.*" By **Unknown**

"*She believed she could, so she did.*" By **R.S. Grey**

"*I'm proud of the woman I am because I went through one hell of a time becoming her.*" By **Unknown**

"*The circles of women in our lives weave invisible nets of love that carry us when we are weak, and they sing with us when we are strong.*" By **Sark**

"Behind every successful woman is a tribe of other successful women, who have her back." By **Kimberly**

"Women should empower each other, instead of being so hateful and envious of one another." By **Unknown**

"A successful woman is one who can build a firm foundation with the bricks others have thrown to her." By **Unknown**

"It took me quite a long time to develop a voice, and now that I have it I am not going to be silent." By **Madeleine Albright**

"She overcomes everything that was meant to destroy her." By **Sylvester McNutt III**

"When women support each other, incredible things happen." By **Viola Davis**

"Each time a woman stands up for herself, she stands up for all women." By **Maya Angelou**

"A woman is unstoppable after she realizes she deserves better." By **Yene D.**

"I am obsessed with seeing women encourage, support, and empower other women. It's my favorite, we need more of it." By **Unknown**

"I would like to be known as an intelligent woman, a courageous woman, a loving woman, a woman who teaches by being." By **Maya Angelou**

"Here's to strong women, may we know them, may we be them, may we raise them." By **Unknown**

"She never seemed shattered; to me she was the breathtaking mosaic of the battles she won." By **Unknown**

"A strong woman, looks a challenge in the eye, and gives it a wink." By **Gina Carey**

"Never underestimate the power of a kind woman. Kindness is a choice that comes from incredible strength." By **Unknown**

"She surrounds herself with women she can grow with." By **Unknown**

"When a woman is loved correctly, she becomes ten times, the woman she was before." By **Unknown**

"A woman unaffected by insult has made her enemies absolutely powerless." By **Entity**

"A strong woman in her essence is a gift to the world." By **Unknown**

"I want every girl to know that her voice can change the world." By **Malala Yousafzai**

"Women who compliment other women genuinely are a whole different breed. Real Queens" By **Unknown**

"Nothing is more impressive than a woman who is secure in the unique way God made her." By **Rhonda Kulczyk**

"Empowered women empower women." By **Unknown**

"A foolish woman keeps talking, a wise woman understands the power of her words as well as her silence." By **Unknown**

"And one day she discovered, that she was fierce, and strong, and full of fire, and that not even she could hold herself back, because her passion burned brighter than her fears." By **Mark Anthony**

"We need women who are so strong, they can be gentle, so educated they can be humble, so fierce they can be compassionate, so passionate they can be rational, and so disciplined they can be free." By **Kavita N. Ramdas**

"A strong woman is a woman determined to do something others are determined not to be done." By **Marge Piercy**

"Be strong enough to let go, and wise enough to wait for what you deserve." By **Unknown**

"Strong women lift each other up." By **Unknown**

"A woman is like a tea bag, you never know how strong it is until it is in hot water." By **Eleanor Roosevelt**

"A strong woman is one, who feels deeply and loves fiercely, her tears flow just as abundantly as her laughter. A strong woman is both soft and powerful, she is both practical and spiritual, a strong woman in her essence is a gift to the world." By **Unknown**

"Strong women wear their pain like stilettos, no matter how much it hurts, all you see is the beauty of it. By **Harriet Morgan**

"Success isn't about how much money you make, it's about the difference you make in people's lives." By **Michelle Obama**

"To attract money, you must focus on wealth. It is impossible, to bring more money into your life, when you are noticing you don't have enough because that means you are thinking thoughts that you don't have enough." By **Rhonda Byrne**

"You can only become truly accomplished at something you love. Don't make money your goal. Instead pursue the things you love doing and then do them so well that people can't take their eyes off you." By **Maya Angelou**

"Here's to financially independent Women, may we know them, may we be them, may we raise them." By **Unknown**

"People, who have drawn wealth into their lives, used the secret consciously or unconsciously, they think thoughts of abundance of

wealth, and they don't allow any contradictory to take roots in their minds." By **Rhonda Byrne**

"Save your money and one day your money will save you." By **Unknown**

"Nearly every glamorous, wealthy, successful career woman, you might envy now, started out as some kind of schlep. By **Helen Gurley Brown**

"A business career for a woman, and her needs for a woman's life, as wife and mother, are not enemies at all, unless we make them so. But maybe the closest and most co-operative friends and supporters of each other." By **Hortense Oldum**

"Leadership is about making others better as a result of your presence and making sure that impact lasts in your absence." By **Sheryl Sandberg**

"Women need to shift from thinking I'm not ready to do that to I'll learn by doing it." By **Sheryl Sandberg**

"If your actions create a legacy that inspires others to dream more, learn more, do more and become more, then, you are an excellent leader." By **Dolly Parton**

"I just want women to always feel in control, because we are capable, we're so capable." By **Nicki Minaj**

"A leader takes people where they want to go. A great leader takes people where they don't necessarily want to go, but ought to be." By **Rosalynn Carter**

"Because I am a woman, I must make unusual effort to succeed. If I fail, no one will say, 'She doesn't have what it takes.' They will say, women don't have what it takes." By **Unknown**

"*Our deepest fear is not that we are inadequate. Our deepest fear is that we are powerful beyond measure.*" By **Marianne Williamson**

"*Leadership is hard to define and good leadership even harder. But if you can get people to follow you to the end of the earth, you are a great leader.*" By **Indra Nooyi**

"*People respond well to those that are sure of what they want.*" By **Anna Wintour**

"*No power on earth compares to a mother's tender prayer.*" By **Edwin Arnold**

"*I remember my mother's prayer and they have always followed me. They have clung to me all my life.*" By **Abraham Lincoln**

"*The battle for our children's lives is waged on our knees.*" By **Stormie Omartian**

"*Prayer warrior mothers cover their kids with God's blessings and protection.*" By **Marla Alupoaicei**

"*Every mother's prayer; guide her to a place where she'll be safe.*" By **Carole Bayer Sager**

"*The bond between mothers and their children is one defined by love. As a mother's prayer for her children are unending, so are the wisdom, grace and strength they provide for their children.*" By **President George W. Bush**

"*God does hear and answer prayers. . . From childhood, at my mother's knee where I first learned to pray . . . I know without question that it is possible for men and women to reach out in humility and prayer and tap that Unseen Power.*" ~ **Ezra Taft Benson**

"*During all those years of struggle and heartache, my mother never worried. She took all her troubles to God in prayer.*" ~**Dale Carnegie**

"My mother knew when to listen and when to pray and when to help. I wonder how many people knew the compassion [my mother] held for them and how hard, in the privacy of her God Box, she prayed for them and their struggles." **~Mary Lou Quinlan**

"To this day, even though I am grown and have two children of my own, whenever I travel somewhere distant or am undertaking a major project, my mother will sit me down, lay hands on me, and say a prayer of blessing." **~Francisco J. García** Jr.

"From the time of my earliest memories, she impressed upon me one rule above all others: when I woke from sleep, my first duty was to pray to God for spiritual nourishment and blessings . . . my mother would never relent . . . She planted in me, and tended in my early life, a profound love and fear of God." **~Sadhu Sundar Singh**

<u>Bible Wisdom About the Woman of Destiny</u>

Proverbs 31:30;"Charm is deceitful and beauty is passing, But a woman who fears the LORD, she shall be praised."

Psalm 46:5 "God is in the midst of her, she shall not be moved; God shall help her, just at the break of dawn."

Proverbs 31:16-17 "She considers a field and buys it; from her profits she plants a vineyard. She girds herself with strength, and strengthens her arms."

1 Corinthians 15:10 "But by the grace of God I am what I am, and His grace toward me was not in vain; but I labored more abundantly than they all, yet not I, but the grace of God *which was* with me."

Proverbs 31:20-21 "She extends her hand to the poor, Yes, she reaches out her hands to the needy. She is not afraid of snow for her household, For all her household *is* clothed with scarlet."

Psalm 139:14 "I will praise You, for I am fearfully and wonderfully made; Marvellous are Your works, And that my soul knows very well."

1 Corinthians 11:12 "For as woman came from man, even so man also comes through woman; but all things are from God."

1 Peter 3:3-4 "Do not let your adornment be merely outward—arranging the hair, wearing gold, or putting on fine apparel—rather let it be the hidden person of the heart, with the incorruptible beauty of a gentle and quiet spirit, which is very precious in the sight of God."

1 Timothy 3:11 "Likewise, their wives must be reverent, not slanderers, temperate, faithful in all things."

Luke 1:45 "Blessed is she who believed that there will be a fulfilment of those things which were told her from the Lord."

Proverbs.31:20 "She extends her hand to the poor, Yes, she reaches out her hands to the needy."

Proverbs 11:16 "A gracious woman retains honor, But ruthless *men* retain riches."

Proverbs 31:25 "Strength and honor *are* her clothing; She shall rejoice in time to come."

Proverbs 3:15 "She *is* more precious than rubies, And all the things you may desire cannot compare with her."

Proverbs 31:26 " She opens her mouth with wisdom, And on her tongue *is* the law of kindness.."

Proverbs. 14:1 "The wise woman builds her house, But the foolish pulls it down with her hands.

Proverbs. 19:13 "A foolish son is the ruin of his father, And the contentions of a wife are a continual dripping."

Proverbs. 21:9 "Better to dwell in a corner of a housetop, Than in a house shared with a contentious woman."

Proverbs. 31: 17–18 "She girds herself with strength, And strengthens her arms. She perceives that her merchandise is good, And her lamp does not go out by night."

Proverbs.21:19 "Better to dwell in the wilderness, Than with a contentious and angry woman."

Proverbs. 31: 16 "She considers a field and buys it; From her profits she plants a vineyard."

Proverbs.12:4 "An excellent wife is the crown of her husband, But she who causes shame is like rottenness in his bones."

Proverbs. 31:19 "She stretches out her hands to the distaff, And her hand holds the spindle.

Proverbs. 31:10–12 "Who can find a virtuous wife? For her worth is far above rubies. The heart of her husband safely trusts her; So he will have no lack of gain. She does him good and not evil All the days of her life."

Proverbs. 31:13–15 "She seeks wool and flax, And willingly works with her hands. She is like the merchant ships, She brings her food from afar. She also rises while it is yet night, And provides food for her household, And a portion for her maidservants."

Proverbs.31:26 "She opens her mouth with wisdom, And on her tongue is the law of kindness."

Ephesians.5:22-23 "Wives, submit to your own husbands, as to the Lord. For the husband is head of the wife, as also Christ is head of the church; and He is the Savior of the body."

1ˢᵗ Peter. 3:1-2 "Wives, likewise, be submissive to your own husbands, that even if some do not obey the word, they, without a word, may be won by the conduct of their wives, when they observe your chaste conduct accompanied by fear."

Titus. 2:3-5 "The older women likewise, that they be reverent in behaviour, not slanderers, not given to much wine, teachers of good things— that they admonish the young women to love their husbands, to love their children to be discreet, chaste, homemakers, good, obedient to their own husbands, that the word of God may not be blasphemed."

1ˢᵗ Tim. 2:9-10 "In like manner also, that the women adorn themselves in modest apparel, with propriety and moderation, not with braided hair or gold or pearls or costly clothing, but, which is proper for women professing godliness, with good works."

1ˢᵗ Cor. 11:3 "But I want you to know that the head of every man is Christ, the head of woman is man, and the head of Christ is God."

1ˢᵗ Tim.5:14 "Therefore I desire that the younger widows marry, bear children, manage the house, give no opportunity to the adversary to speak reproachfully."

Col.3:18-19 "Wives, submit to your own husbands, as is fitting in the Lord. Husbands, love your wives and do not be bitter toward them."

Proverbs.31:27 "She watches over the ways of her household, And does not eat the bread of idleness."

2ⁿᵈ Tim.1:5 "when I call to remembrance the genuine faith that is in you, which dwelt first in your grandmother Lois and your mother Eunice, and I am persuaded is in you also."

Proverbs.31:28 "Her children rise up and call her blessed; Her husband also, and he praises her."

Proverbs.31:25 "Strength and honour are her clothing; She shall rejoice in time to come."

Proverbs 18:22 "He who finds a wife finds a good thing, And obtains favour from the LORD."

Proverbs.23:22 "Listen to your father who begot you, And do not despise your mother when she is old."

Proverbs.4:6 "Do not forsake her, and she will preserve you; Love her, and she will keep you."

Proverbs.11:22 "As a ring of gold in a swine's snout, So is a lovely woman who lacks discretion."

Proverbs.31:21 "She is not afraid of snow for her household, For all her household is clothed with scarlet."

Bibliography

The Bible

Jakes, T.D.2002. *God's Leading Lady: Out of the Shadows and into the Light.* Berkley.

Sandberg, Sheryl & Scovell, Nell.2013. *Lean In: Women, Work, and the Will to Lead.* Alfred A. Knopf.

Stigel, V. Herta.2011. *The Mountain Within: Leadership Lessons and Inspiration for Your Climb to the Top.* McGraw-Hill Eductaion.

Scott, Janny.2011. *A Singular Woman: The Untold Story of Barack Obama's Mother.* Riverhead Books.

Meyer, Joyce.2010. *Eat the Cookie... Buy the Shoes: Giving Yourself Permission to Lighten Up.* FaithWords.

Karssen, Gien.1974. *Her Name is Woman.* NavPress Publishing Group.

Live By Faith by Rev. Teresa Wairimu

Yancey, Philip.2002. *Where Is God When It Hurts?* Zondervan.

Shellenberger, Susie & Gowler, Kathy.2007. *What Your Daughter Isn't Telling You: Expert Insight Into the World of Teen Girls.* Bethany House Publishers.

Boundaries by Pastor Sammy Hinn

Covey, R. Stephen. 2004. The *7 Habits of Highly Effective People: Powerful Lessons in Personal Change.* Free Press.

Dr. D. W. Ekstrand, 2012. The Influence Parents have on their Children. Accessed on 28th July, 2020 http://www.thetransformedsoul.com/additional-studies

Sasha, 2016: The influence of a good teacher can never be erased. Accessed on 28th July, 2020 https://mirrorgirlblog.wordpress.com/2016/09/17/

Leslie Becker-Phelps, PHD, 2005; Ways your Friends Influence your Future. Accessed on https://blogs.webmd.com/relationships/20160928

Brandon Thomas, 2008: Does past experience affect what we see or what we do? accessed on 29th July, 2020 https://www.researchgate.net/post/Does_past_experience

Art Markman, Ph.D. 2011: Your View of the Future Is Shaped by the Past. Accessed on 29th July, 2020 https://www.psychologytoday.com/us/blog/ulterior-motives/201108

Orit E. Tykocinski and Andreas Ortmann. 2011: The Lingering Effects of Our Past Experiences: The Sunk-Cost Fallacy and the Inaction-Inertia Effect. Accessed on 29th July, 2020 http://portal.idc.ac.il/he/schools/psychology/

Claire Newton. 2020: Destiny: Action or Accident? Accessed on 29th July 2020 http://www.clairenewton.co.za/my-articles/destiny-action-or-accident.html

Sandra Dawes.2014. Following your inner voice. Accessed on 29th July, 2020 https://embraceurdestiny.com/2014/01/29/

following-your inner-voice/

Kenneth Copeland, 2018. Ways to Know If You're Hearing God's Voice. Accessed on 29th July,2020 https://blog.kcm.org/4-ways-know-youre-hearing-gods-voice/

Pincott Jena E, 2019. Silencing Your Inner Critic, accessed on 29th July, 2020 https://www.psychologytoday.com/us/articles/201903/silencing-your-inner-critic

Bonnie Badenoch, Ph.D. 2010. Critical Inner Voice. Accessed on 29th July, 2020 https://www.psychalive.org/critical-inner-voice/

www.ingramcontent.com/pod-product-compliance
Lightning Source LLC
Chambersburg PA
CBHW071734150726

47998CB00005B/1636